By the same author:

Brother Whale

Lahaina—Royal Capital of Hawaii

Hawaii: The Volcano State

Robert Lewis Stevenson in California

Sea Otters: A Natural History and Guide

The Friendly Whales

The Friendly Whales

A WHALEWATCHER'S GUIDE TO
THE GRAY WHALES
OF BAJA CALIFORNIA

ROY NICKERSON

CHRONICLE BOOKS • SAN FRANCISCO

Library of Congress Cataloging-in-Publication Data

Nickerson, Roy.
  The friendly whales.

  Bibliography: p. 115
  Includes index.
  1. Pacific gray whale. 2. Pacific gray whale—Behavior.
3. Mammals—Behavior. 4. Mammals—Mexico—
Baja California. I. Title.
QL737.C425N53 1987   599.5′1   87-728
ISBN 0-87701-374-8 (pbk.)

All photographs by the author, except:
Cover: Marc Webber
Page 5: National Weather Service, Redwood City office
Page 13: Bancroft Library
Page 18: Robert Fish, *Monterey Peninsula Herald*
Page 27: Archives of Hawaii
Page 48: Sea World, San Diego
Page 109: Sea Life Park, Oahu

Editing: Deborah Stone
Book and cover design: Naomi Schiff
Typography: TBH/Typecast, Inc., Cotati

10 9 8 7 6 5 4 3 2 1

Chronicle Books
One Hallidie Plaza
San Francisco, CA 94102

Table of Contents

Acknowledgements

A NUMBER OF BUSY PROFESSIONALS in the field I am writing about have taken time out to help me gather facts or to read over portions of my original manuscript and make corrections or suggestions. Among these I am especially grateful to Drs. Howard W. Braham and Marilyn Dahlheim, National Marine Fisheries Service (NMFS), National Marine Mammal Laboratory, Seattle; Dr. Luis A. Fleischer, Centro de Investigaciones Pesqueras, La Paz, Baja California Sur; Norman A. Mendes, Chief, Tuna/Porpoise Management Branch, NMFS, San Diego; Al Molina, naturalist and biology instructor, College of Marin; Dr. Kenneth S. Norris, Environmental Field Program, University of California, Santa Cruz; Dr. William Perrin, NMFS, Southwest Fisheries Center, La Jolla; Dana J. Seagars, wildlife biologist, NMFS, Terminal Island, California; Dr. Elizabeth F. Vetter, NMFS, Southwest Fisheries Center, La Jolla; Dr. Steven K. Webster, Director of Education, Monterey Bay Aquarium, Monterey.

The following publishers have kindly granted permission to quote from their books and authors: William Morrow & Company, excerpts from *Hunting the Desert Whale,* by Erle Stanley Gardner; Nantucket Historical Association, excerpts from *The Loss of the Ship Essex,* by Thomas Nickerson; Natural History Museum of Los Angeles County, excerpts from "The Friendly Whales of Laguna San Ignacio," by Raymond Gilmore, *Terra*, Vol. 15, No. 1; California Academy of Sciences, excerpt from "The Friendly Whale," by George Lindsay, *Pacific Discovery*, Vol. 31, No. 6. Dover Publications has been helpful with Capt. Charles M. Scammon's work, which is in the public domain. Publishing convention allows brief quotes of copyrighted material without specific permission, but I wish to acknowledge references to the writings of the late Dr. Joseph Wood Krutch, William Morrow & Co., Publishers; and of John Steinbeck, Viking Penguin and the author's heirs.

I have received valuable assistance from various staff members of the American Cetacean Society; the International Whaling Commission; the Marine Mammal Commission; Sea World, San Diego and Orlando; The Whale Center, Oakland; and the library of the Monterey Bay Aquarium. Christopher Barnes of Carmel has been helpful with his suggestions and work on the Baja California map.

Robin Lee Makowski's original artwork has greatly enhanced this book, providing details which could never be photographed.

Introduction

TO ANYONE WHO HAS COME TO CHERISH the existence of the family of whales, from the tiny harbor porpoise to the mighty blue whale, the lagoons of Baja California eventually become the object of pilgrimage. Like the once-in-a-lifetime visit to Mecca for the Bedouin of Araby or the Sahara Desert, the journey is not always possible. But it remains a dream that kindles hope.

It is my good fortune to have been able to make a number of trips to the Baja California peninsula and two specifically to San Ignacio Lagoon. Here I have taken part in the "friendly" whale phenomenon. Some old salts refer to the grays in those lagoons as "curious" rather than "friendly" whales; curiosity may be the key to what started this contact between whales and people back in the mid-1970s. Now this activity shows signs of spreading to other parts of the Pacific west coast.

The whales, of course, aren't the only curious ones. Visits to the lagoons are popular with scientists, with amateur naturalists and with whalewatchers.

The whale family has been the subject of a veritable explosion of writing over the past two decades. Trained scientists, specialist with Ph.D.s and funded researchers have found themselves sharing the shelves with amateur, largely self-taught naturalists such as myself. The true academicians have accommodated us with good grace. Others have been a bit huffy about it. There is plenty of room for both amateur and specialist. The scientist, after all, tends to explore a single subject and to publish either for fellow scientists or for students on the way to joining academic ranks. The naturalist can write more generally, more entertainingly and, perhaps, more worshipfully.

Over the years a half-dozen scientists and writers have beckoned me along the naturalist's path. John Steinbeck was one of them; he may have been the least patient of them all with the trained expert. In *The Log From the Sea of Cortez* he wrote:

> There is a curious idea among unscientific men that in scientific writing there is a common plateau of perfectionism. Nothing could be more untrue. The reports of biologists are the measure, not of the science, but of the men themselves . . . A dull man seems to be a dull man no matter what his field, and of course it is the right of a dull scientist to protect himself with feathers and robes, emblems and degrees, as do other dull men who are potentates and grand imperial rulers of lodges of dull men.

My own favorite writer of nature was the late Dr. Joseph Wood Krutch, whom I knew briefly when I lived in Tucson in the late 1950s and whose degree was not in science. In *The Forgotten Peninsula,* he wrote:

> Your amateur . . . is delightfully, if not almost sinfully, free of responsibility and can spread himself as thin as he likes over the vast field of nature . . . Best of all, perhaps, is the fact that he feels no pressing obligation to "add something to the sum of human knowledge." And if he keeps his field wide enough he will remain so ignorant that he may do exactly that at intervals very gratifyingly short . . .
>
> . . . to the amateur, any flower he has never seen before is a new species as far as he is concerned and on a short trip into a new area he can easily find a dozen "new species."

Dr. Krutch, who died in 1970 at the age of 77, started his professional career as a professor of English literature and journalism and drama and was eventually pleased to combine all three talents to produce

A skiff party prepares to leave Qualifier *to circle Los Islotes to view sea lions, frigate birds and brown boobies nesting in the pinnacles' rocks.*

some of America's finest nature writing. In the process he influenced a number of people who remain grateful to him years after his death. I am one of them.

The earliest scientific writer to describe areas I was later to visit myself was the late Dr. William Beebe. For many years he was the director

The Friendly Whales

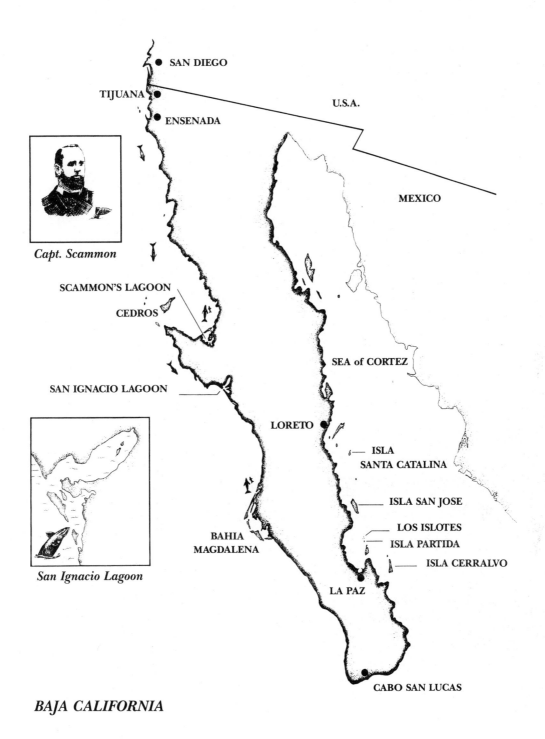

SAN DIEGO

TIJUANA

U.S.A.

ENSENADA

Capt. Scammon

MEXICO

SCAMMON'S LAGOON

CEDROS

SEA of CORTEZ

SAN IGNACIO LAGOON

LORETO

ISLA
SANTA CATALINA

ISLA SAN JOSE

LOS ISLOTES

BAHIA
MAGDALENA

ISLA PARTIDA

ISLA CERRALVO

San Ignacio Lagoon

LA PAZ

CABO SAN LUCAS

BAJA CALIFORNIA

of the Department of Tropical Research of the New York Zoological Society. His book, *Zaca Venture*, published in 1938, became an early bible to me.

The *Zaca* was a beautiful yacht, a two-masted schooner with diesel auxiliary, owned by Templeton Crocker. He placed his yacht, himself and crew at Dr. Beebe's disposal in 1936 for a scientific cruise through the waters surrounding Baja California. Dr. Beebe was especially fascinated with Cedros Island, off Baja California's Pacific coast. When I finally visited there recently, I was at least as much in awe of the place as any of the Faithful would be of Mecca. I brought back with me some small stones that really should be strung as holy beads.

It seems to me that my visits to Baja California have had a lifetime of preparation. My own voyages there started as Steinbeck's did, from Monterey. When Steinbeck hired a fishing boat in 1940, he did so because his biologist friend—whom he immortalized as Doc Ricketts in *Cannery Row*—was a collector of biological specimens.

The lure for both Ricketts, the scientist, and Steinbeck, the amateur naturalist, was the wealth of unnamed and unexamined specimens awaiting them in Baja California. Perhaps not completely unnamed and unexamined: a predecessor of Dr. Beebe was John Xantus, a Hungarian who went to Baja California in 1859. He spent 28 months there and found some 300 species of birds, insects and inhabitants of tidepools that scientists had never seen before. A number of them today include *xantii* or *xantusiana* as the second half of their Latin description in recognition of his efforts. The result of their voyage to the Sea of Cortez was the book *The Sea of Cortez*. Although Ricketts studied zoology at the University of Chicago, he did not finalize his academic career formally; it remained for Steinbeck to award him the title *Doc*. Even without the Ph.D., a number of critters in science today end with *rickettsi*!

I think the greatest thing I hope to accomplish is to add to the growing awareness of the whales, the world they live in and the marine mammals they share their space with. As a writer, I am in a crowded field! But I have been deeply and permanently touched by the marine mammals. And I feel the world is in good shape as long as the human race is capable of the compassion necessary to work for the salvation of the whales. If we can't save the whales, then I don't think we can save ourselves.

Roy Nickerson
Carmel

CHAPTER ONE

To Begin With

"EIGHTEEN FEET." THE CREWMAN'S VOICE SQUAWKED over the portable CB from the small skiff he was riding a hundred yards ahead of us.

"It's going to get a lot shallower than that real fast," the captain shot back. "Turn right."

We were aboard the *Qualifier–105*, a motor vessel powered by three diesel engines that carried me—along with 30 other amateur naturalists—on my first of several voyages to San Ignacio Lagoon. This particular trip was the most exciting of them all; the first time always is.

"We're over a sandbar," the crewman's voice came. It carried just a tinge of excitement. He'd scouted the entrance to the lagoon many times before, but there was always a newness to the task. "It's only six feet."

Capt. John Grabowski turned the wheel hard and the *Qualifier* stayed in bluer waters.

"Change course again. It's shallower to the right," he radioed the crewman.

From the bridge the captain had a better view of where the water was shallow and where it was deeper. He just couldn't tell how shallow or how deep.

"Gotcha," came back the word from the skiff. "It's just dropped back to 16."

The captain turned the *Q105* in that direction. We were going forward, but not at full speed.

San Ignacio is one of the lagoons where the Pacific gray whales guarded the secret of their existence until that fateful day when whaling captain Charles Melville Scammon stumbled onto them—and led the onslaught against them to the brink of eternity. Always changing, the entrance to the lagoon was especially treacherous now because the tide was out. The pure sand bottom and the strong and erratic currents make it impossible to chart the entrance with any degree of permanence. This, of course, is what also saved the whales of Baja California for long enough to allow them to recover from near-oblivion.

The hour of departure was early for this trip, my first to San Ignacio Lagoon. San Diego Harbor was completely colorless at that hour of the morning—unless you include gray as a color. Passing the civilian yachting fleet and ships from America's war-and-peace fleet that dwarfed us all, we left Point Loma and headed to sea in a southwesterly direction.

Early the next morning we were close to the Baja California shore, which from this distance looked like a big sand dune. Behind the dune, a jagged purple mountain range in the distance rose from the morning mists to saw at the deep blue sky above.

Nowhere was there a hint of a lagoon, let alone the entrance to one.

But the whales were there. We met them in small groups of two and three, even singly. Some whales voyaged north; at points of meeting, the skipper slipped the engines into idle for a moment. Giving us what appeared to be a startled look, the passing whales would settle from view below the surface, then come straight up, head and eyes appearing slowly out of the water. This position we humans call *spyhopping*. Although the whales were curious, friendly people-watchers, they paused only a brief second in their journey north, sometimes pausing again a few hundred yards away for a final spyhop.

While whales and people watched each other, the captain headed our ship toward disaster. Dark blue water gave way to light blue, and at moments to the white-green hue of dangerously shallow water. I tried not to be unnerved, for I had complete faith in the skipper—even though he looked little older than a high school athlete. (As the years pass, ships' captains and their crews look younger and younger to me.)

Someone has to keep the faith; it might as well be me.

Sure enough, without there actually appearing to be an entryway at first, the sand did give way to the ship's progress. Then water began to wash over the sands and finally, indistinct at first, a passage opened.

At that moment I understood how startled the sailor in the lookout of Captain Scammon's sailing vessel a century ago must have been, absently scanning endless sand dunes, when he spotted the unmistakable spouting of a whale from their very center.

Our captain had a skiff with two crewmen running ahead of us. One man sat on the outboard motor and gingerly steered according to instructions repeated by the other crew member, who had a portable fathometer between his legs and a CB link with the skipper pressed against his ear and mouth.

"Eighteen feet," the lead man called.

"Hold steady," the captain radioed back. The man astride the outboard nodded agreement to his skiffmate.

"Fifteen feet."

"Twelve feet."

"Nine feet."

We gathered on the bridge and held our breath. Even though the ship drew only six feet, we all felt she needed more.

The depth shot back to 14 feet, then 12, then 15, then never less than 12 again. An angel passing overhead watching our zigzag wake and not knowing what we were up to would have sworn that we were leading the life of a drunken sailor.

For the next several hundred yards the water remained green tinged with telltale sandy, cloudy white. Without the men in the skiff running before us, we would have beached ourselves a dozen times, just as whalers of the past century did, powered only by wind and at the mercy of sudden and unpredictable shifts of the elements.

"All right," the captain radioed, "from now on, bear to the right to deeper water."

Finally, as if the sandy barrier had not existed at all, we were inside Laguna San Ignacio and sailing free.

Captain Scammon's first lagoon was Laguna Ojo de Liebre — Jackrabbit Spring Lagoon — perhaps 75 miles to the north of San Ignacio by land but three times that distance by sea because of a sudden outjutting of land called Punta San Eugenio. (Scammon also found another smaller lagoon running into Ojo de Liebre to the north,

Pelicans fly in formation at San Ignacio Lagoon.

Guerrero Negro Lagoon). Ojo de Liebre now bears the captain's name in most books and on most maps: Scammon's Lagoon.

These lagoons are now closed to most traffic. The Mexican Government has had the foresight to establish the world's first whale sanctuary at Scammon's Lagoon and has placed most of Laguna San Ignacio off limits to casual visitors. Entry to San Ignacio is strictly controlled, but limited numbers are allowed by permit.

We crossed Laguna San Ignacio in less than half an hour, reaching a spit of land called Rocky Point. Here we anchored, barred by law from going any farther.

Beyond this point are the main gray whale nurseries. Here mothers mate one year and return the next to give birth. The waters are shallow and warm and extra salty, making them more buoyant than the open sea and providing the perfect cradle for the baby gray whale.

The lagoons mark the midpoint of an extraordinary migration—a journey the grays make every year—a round trip totaling some 12,000 miles. It is the longest known migration of any animal. Only the humpback whales' annual trip from the inlets of Alaska to the Hawaiian Islands and back is close to this phenomenon.

Captain Scammon painted this watercolor of whaling in Scammon's Lagoon.

It also seems that the mother gray whales have learned—here—that humans no longer come in boats to kill them. Perhaps because whaling of the grays in the northeast Pacific has been outlawed for so long, the only whales with reason to be wary of man and boats are those in Korean and Japanese waters. Scientific observers and tuna fishermen have recently reported that dolphins somehow sense—at least in Mexico's Pacific waters—which boats are tuna boats and which are not. They often flee at the first sound of a purse seiner. It follows that the whales have developed this same understanding and sense that some ships are safe and others pose danger.

From the deck of our ship, I could see the gray whales surface-traveling at a businesslike pace, leaving behind them little puffs of mist. Other whales spyhopped: An occasional gray hurled himself completely free of the water and came down with a resounding bellywhopper. One baby gray attempted this trick but managed only a confusion of froth.

The air around us was so charged with excitement we could all feel it. Here I will break off my log of this journey to get in some basic cetology.

CHAPTER TWO

The Whale In Question

THE WHALE WE WILL BE DEALING WITH for the most part in this book is the gray whale, *Eschrichtius robustus.* Visitors to the magic lagoons of Baja California started calling them "the friendlies" back in the mid-1970s; later came the references to "the friendly whale syndrome." Amateur and professional naturalists alike are entranced with this species of whale which, less than a century before, had such a fierce reputation that certain seafarers called them devilfish.

In those days, however, visitors to the lagoons didn't have such friendly intentions. These whalers came to kill as many of the grays as their ships could hold. As we'll soon read in more detail, whalers had no conscience over how they bagged their game. One favorite trick was to harpoon a baby; the 40-ton mother would remain in the area think-ing she could rescue her offspring, giving the whalers time to close in on the mother and secure two or three harpoons deep into her flesh.

They soon learned they did this at their own peril. There is no more protective mother among whales than the gray. In an effort to protect her baby, mother gray rammed skiffs, launches and even the large whal-ing ships themselves. Twelve-foot-wide flukes slamming down on whale boats scarcely twice that length quickly turned the hunter into the hunted. Devilfish was as good a name as any to call these fierce mother grays.

A visit to the watery domain of the grays means encounters with other types of whales, each as appealing in its own way, though few have exhibited the same friendly behavior the mother grays and their babies have shown in recent years in the lagoons. For the most part, whales mind their own business. Sometimes in areas where they linger for a season and become used to fishing or whalewatching boats, they'll choose to come up for a quick inspection to satisfy their curiosity. In the waters of the Auau Channel between Hawaii's Lanai and Maui, or off Kahoolawe or Maui's Maalaea Bay, I have had the humpbacks come up to a boat I was in and circle about, only yards away, for a half-hour at a time!

And Dr. Roger Payne, the famed researcher with the New York Zoological Society whose fascinating reports have become familiar in *The National Geographic,* also found the right whales off Patagonia to be friendly. He and members of his teams have found themselves swimming within inches of 60-foot rights.

The gray whales also share the waters of the open Pacific of Baja California's west coast with seals and sea lions and fur seals and elephant seals. There are also the largest of whales, the blue whales — and the smallest of whales, the porpoises. There are the in-betweens, the dolphins and sometimes the biggest dolphins, the killer whales.

At one time there were three separate stocks, or groups, of gray whales. The North Atlantic stock was completely wiped out by the 1800s by centuries of whaling. A large western Pacific population of grays found off the coasts of Korea, Japan and parts of eastern Russia has been hunted so ruthlessly, right into contemporary times, that the stock is considered extinct.

"Our" gray whales, we happily report, continue to flourish; the present California gray whale population is estimated to number 17,000. It is thought by scientists that this figure is about the peak number of gray whales that has lived at any one time during their 30 million years of history in the eastern North Pacific Ocean.

Because the population of grays came back to this figure in the early 1980s, the U.S. Fish & Wildlife Service, which enforces the applicable portions of the Marine Mammal Protection Act of 1972, proposed downgrading their status from the "endangered" category to "threatened." While both categories extend protection to whales, the implications of such a reclassification are unfortunate, to say the least. The subliminal message is that it's permissible to start "harvesting"—a charming expression!—the grays again.

Government scientists[1] state that the gray whale is "approaching the carrying capacity" in the part of the world in which they feed. I have often wondered what would happen if some world body—a United Nations with teeth, perhaps—should determine the human "carrying capacity" for different regions of the world. Once that capacity is reached, the laws against murder could be repealed and "harvesting" of the human population permitted.

Apparently the human race has assumed the right to play God with other species.

Both the Marine Mammal Protection Act and the Endangered Species Act of 1973 are designed to protect specified animals and their habitats. This can mean insisting on safeguards at offshore oil drilling sites through which a species of whale, dolphin or other marine mammal may pass or where it may feed. It can and should be enforced to apply to rivers that spill urban pollution into the oceans. Whales now tend to avoid the close contact they once had with such areas as the Los Angeles and San Diego harbors, probably because of pollution spillover. Runoff from coastal farms washes pesticides and fertilizers into the sea; contact with these pollutants destroys the lungs and poisons the flesh of man and beast alike!

Gray whales are especially susceptible to fallout from human behavior because they remain so close to shore. Of all the whales of the world, the grays live closest to man. To visit most whales long boat trips are necessary. Not so the grays; we almost share the same air. And the grays are the most visible of whales. Their remarkable annual migration is witnessed by many thousands who need never board a whalewatching boat. From vantage points along the Pacific Coast from the state of Washington to southern California, entranced humans watch the parade of spouts and gleaming backs by the hour.

The best whalewatching is along the California coast, where the grays hug the shore. Humans return year after year to the same knolls and

---

1. I refer to goverment scientists above; actually not all are in the employ of a government. Some may be temporarily in the service of government, serving on appointed panels such as delegations to International Whaling Commission conferences, which annually set up "kill quotas" for the few remaining whaling nations.

Gray whales rise to the surface and blow during their migration south along the California coast.

hillocks and beaches, just as year after year the grays return to the lagoons of Baja California. Whalewatching boats need not venture far from their departure points during migration months to make contact.

As used to this activity as I am, however, I was completely unprepared for a sighting I had recently. Friends of mine visiting Carmel, where I live, rented a house on the rocks at the very edge of Carmel Bay. One day I looked out their window and saw a gray whale swimming at the very edge of a kelp bed less than 300 yards away.

Gray whales are what are known as "bottom grazers," preferring less than 200 feet of water. They eat squid, the kind California fishermen use for bait, among other things. Or they will also swim through a school of small fish, mouth wide open; slamming their jaws shut, they trap their lunch behind their net of baleen. They will even take in the small pelagic crabs (known as lobster krill to fishermen) we sometimes see in harbors, or along the shore after storms at sea or during periods of especially warm water.

Gray whales belong to the family of whales without teeth. They cannot chase and grab onto something like the sperm whale, the orca (or killer whale), or dolphins, porpoises and other toothed whales. The humpback, the fin whale, the right and the blue whale all have these same great sievelike curtains hanging at the front of their mouths. The food is trapped inside.

Most often gray whales dive in shallow-bottom seas and inlets, coves and river mouths, sucking up great mouthfuls of amphipods—the small crustaceans living on the ocean floor in sand and fine pebbles. These pebbles will sometimes find their way into the whales' stomachs. Sand, invertebrates and all are sucked into the huge mouth, helped by the two to four grooves the gray has in its throat to allow accordion-like expansion when the mouth is full. Bringing forth its tremendous tongue, the whale forces forward everything it took in and extrudes water and finer particles back through the baleen.

Once the tongue has forced the water out, the whale swallows whatever food it has taken in and makes another dive to the bottom for more. Cetologists have found that the gray turns sideways to make its pass along the ocean bottom, almost always on its left side, leaving the left side of its face scraped somewhat free of the barnacles and other infestations its body is subject to.

Baleen whales are known to cetologists as *mysticetes,* a word which has its roots in the Greek word for moustache—a reference to the baleen. The gray whale belongs to a family by itself, called Eschritiidae after a nineteenth century German zoologist, D. F. Eschricht, who described the gray whale most accurately.

The gray is the most primitive of the modern whales: this merely means that they have undergone fewer physical changes since branching off from their common ancestor, the Archeoceti. (This ancient pre-whale is said to have looked more like a sea serpent than the cetaceans we are used to seeing today.) While the grays are thought to have evolved in their present form some 25 million years ago, other whales may have assumed their familiar looks as recently as 10 to 12 million years ago.

Modern whales in the moustache family include the right and the bowhead whales, which don't have throat or stomach grooves; the Balaenopteridae, also called rorqual whales, which can have up to 100 grooves (the blue whale, the fin whale, the sei, and Bryde's and minke whales are all rorqual whales); and the Odontoceti, which have teeth.

The humpback whale's sensory bumps on his rostrum and the high ridge protecting the blowholes are easily seen in this photo.

The magnificent sperm whale, which averages up to 70 feet in length when fully grown, and the little whales, porpoises and dolphins, which can be as small as four feet long, are toothed whales.

Cetaceans breathe air, just as we do. When early whales left land and returned to the water, among the body changes that took place was the migration of the nostrils from the front of the head to the top. Whales' bodies adapted in this way so that they could swim forward effortlessly and not take in water. The nostrils that evolved—called blowholes— have a little ridge to the front and along the side that keeps water from entering the blowhole while the whale travels along the water's surface. Powerful muscles around the blowhole contract to shut the hole when the whale dives; these muscles are relaxed when the whale surfaces and exhales. That exhalation, by the way, creates the familiar spout; this spout is a condensation of inhaled air hitting the atmosphere which combines with water trapped atop the whale's head around the blowholes.

Experienced whalewatchers, like the whalers of old, can tell one whale from another at a distance by the shape of the "blow" or "spout." The shape of this misty cloud is determined by the size of the whale and the number of blowholes it has. Baleen whales have two blowholes,

The humpback is the most playful of the great whales and enjoys flinging his armlike flukes up to enhance a leap from the sea.

while the toothed whales, including dolphins and porpoises, have one. The spout of the gray whale can rise 12 to 15 feet and seems to merge into a single heart-shaped blow. The right whale, also with two blowholes, exhales a very definite V; the sperm whale, with one, puffs forward and to one side and higher than most other whales. I have seen dolphins spout, but these are usually pitiful efforts resembling a sneeze.

A book of this sort has no business conducting a complete class in whale anatomy, but there are a couple further points of interest before we pass on to other things. First, a whale's tail, called the *flukes,* does not move from side to side as does the tail of a fish but is instead worked up and down. And it is worked mightily. An average, leisurely swimming pace for most whales seems to be 4 knots. The fin whale can sustain 20 knots for a period of time, and the blue whale can hit 30, which makes it the fastest-swimming whale. Grays average 4 knots during their long migration. Whales develop sudden and swift bursts of speed for the purpose of feeding on swimming prey.

The most remarkable feat of strength exerted by the flukes is demonstrated by humpbacks, and to a lesser degree by the grays, when they breach. Both can, with two or three powerful strokes of the flukes, propel themselves completely out of the water, landing on their back and sometimes on their side. With less energetic attempts, they flop back down on their stomach. Divers have watched this activity among humpbacks fron. underwater and have verified that only two or three strokes are needed to develop enough power to clear the surface.

Second, most whales have a dorsal fin of sorts, though some do not. The humpback, the blue, the fin, the sei, Bryde's and the minke whale all have a dorsal fin; the right whale and the bowhead do not. The gray whale has instead a row of nine to fourteen bumps, referred to as knuckles. These are not attached to the skeleton or to any muscles; some cetologists hazard the guess that they may have some hydrodynamic function.

Finally, a look at a whale's skeleton reveals hand and foot bones that are hauntingly human. Over eons, these fused and have become single flukes or flippers.

To the Brink and Back

THE CALIFORNIA GRAY WHALE HAS TEETERED on the brink of extinction twice and made a comeback both times. No other whale can make that statement!

Part of the reason for this is the gray's habit of staying so close to shore (their normal range is within a mile of the coast; on the return trip from Baja California to Arctic waters, they sometimes stay a bit farther offshore). The only time they may be out of sight of land is when they traverse a large bight or a bay, such as the Gulf of the Farallons or the southern portion of the California Channel Islands.

Because grays travel alone, in pairs or at the most, in threes, whalers had to work harder to go after them. Humpback whales travel in pods of a half-dozen or more and the sperm whales, the most prized by whalers, are loners. The sperm whales are huge, their 55 and 60 feet packed with both the usual blubber oil and the special spermaceti (oil) found in the case, as the special reservoir located in their head is called.

The right whale (*Balaena glacialis*) was probably the first whale to fall to man's harpoons, swiftly followed by the fin whale (*B. psysalus*). The right whale got its name from early whalers, who knew that of all the whales, these floated the longest after being harpooned; this made

A whaling scene of the 1800s, from Captain Scammon.

them the "right" whale to come upon and kill. Whaling men referred to whales like the humpback as sinkers.

The Norwegians' Norse ancestors were the first whalers. These northern hunters explored the upper Atlantic westward through Iceland and Greenland and the waters off Newfoundland—a world yet unknown— in pursuit of the whale. They ventured south and taught the Basques of southern France and northern Spain the value of the whale. The Basques in turn dominated whaling, eventually chasing the right whale to the shores of the New World. By the year 1,000, the Norse had spread their whalermen across the North Atlantic; the Basques were right behind them less then two centuries later.

The Basques, however, went one step further. Where the Norse started whaling to supply their own people, the Basques began whaling as commerce, dealing in whale products as a means to obtain goods from other nations.

Today Spain—along with China, South Korea, Chile and Portugal—is one of the few nations outside the International Whaling Commission and one of the few to continue a limited amount of whaling.

In modern times the Norwegians carried whaling to the Antarctic. Earlier, in the sixteenth century, they influenced the Dutch and British. The gray whales in the North Atlantic were knocked out of existence completely by the nineteenth century and the right and fin whales were thinned to dangerous lows. The slow but fast-sinking humpback diminished in numbers; early in the present century the North Atlantic population suffered a particularly vicious onslaught when commerce demanded their bodies from which to wring a profitable substitute for butter.

The new United States of America produced the Yankee whalers. These first provisioned at and sailed from Nantucket. New Bedford and other New England ports quickly joined in the commerce. I am sad to say that there were several Captains Nickerson among them!

Captain Scammon recorded the birth and development of Yankee whaling. He writes that the earliest American colonists took up the hunt of the leviathan from the beginning of the 1600s. He quotes Capt. John Smith in Volume II of *Annals of Salem* as reporting that whaling "was one of the first pursuits of the colonial inhabitants of New York and Delaware . . . The right of whale-fishing 'was guaranteed by the Royal Charter of 1629 to the proprietors of Massachusetts, as being within their waters.'"

The captain further writes:

> About 1748, the whales having been driven from the contiguous shores, were pursued farther seaward in sloops and schooners of fifty tons, each of which had a company of thirteen men, and lowered two boats in the chase. In 1765, the whale-fishery from Boston and adjacent ports amounted to one hundred small vessels, which cruised as far to the northward and eastward as the Straits of Belle Isle, the Gulf of St. Lawrence, and to the Western Islands. But at the island of Nantucket, or among the Nantucket men, originated the

grand whaling enterprise which has reached every accessible point around the world.

The Yankee whaling fleet eventually reached the coast of Africa; it also "contended with the ice of Baffin's and Hudson's bays, in search of the mammoth prey, and in open seasons reached the latitude of 81°."

The construction of larger whaling ships in the late 1700s opened up the Pacific to Yankee whalers. In September 1791, "the ship *Rebecca*, owned by those veteran merchants, Joseph Russell & Sons and Cornelius Howland, was among the first, if not the first, of American whalers which doubled Cape Horn and obtained a full cargo in the Pacific."

The *Rebecca*, Scammon wrote, was of 175 tons.

The British had already beat the Yankee whalers to the hunt in the eastern and northern Pacific two years earlier with the *Amalia*, out of London.

The entry of the Yankee whaling fleet into the Pacific had its most immediate impact on sperm whales, already under attack off Asian shores by the Japanese and the Russians, and from shore stations by the native people of Siberia. The right whale population in the North Pacific was nearly wiped out shortly after the nineteenth century got under way. Sightings of them now are so significant that each becomes part of the permanent record. Among those few recorded in recent years was one by the late Dr. Raymond M. Gilmore off the California coast in 1956; on March 25, 1979, I was among a fortunate group of whalewatchers sighting one off Maui, in the Hawaiian Islands, in the company of a pod of humpbacks.

The whalers used the port of Lahaina at Maui—in the midst of humpback winter grounds—to reprovision their ships and to allow their crew to regain their land legs briefly. They didn't carry on too much whaling in Hawaiian waters, but even so the North Pacific humpback population was so reduced that even today it is estimated that no more than 900 individuals remain there.

The search for sperm whales led American whalers to the far ends of the North Pacific, leading to contact with humpbacks, blues and bowheads, and put whalers on a collision course with the grays. Two-ton elephant seals were also sought by whalers for their oil to the extent that, wrote Captain Scammon, "the animals have long since been virtually annihilated." Captain Scammon records that the whaling fleet pushed farther north and dared challenge the ice of the Arctic. Here

The famous Roach Fleet—the ships Enterprise, Wm. Roach, Pocahontas *and* Houqua—*among a pod of sperm whales in the Pacific.*

Eskimos and native Americans had long gone after the whales from their shore stations. The Eskimos went from their villages in boats 25 and 30 feet long with crews of eight made up of both men and women.

Such local subsistence whaling was hardly a threat to whale populations. Today's native Alaskans fight yearly for the right to continue to hunt the bowhead both for subsistence and to preserve this part of their ancient culture. They battle the Internatinal Whaling Commission and the U.S. Government for an annual kill quota that hovers around 30 whales. Unfortunately, the bowhead population is so decimated that even this relatively small amount will probably lead to the extinction of the species.

A far greater menace than subsistence whaling to the northern right whale, the gray, and the bowhead was the advance of the large American

California gray whales in the Bering Sea (from Capt. Charles M. Scammon).

whaling fleet, which numbered some 735 ships of various sizes and descriptions. Some of their number first entered the Bering Sea off Alaska and the Sea of Okhotsk off Siberia in 1843. Thus began the grays' first brush with extinction.

Captain Scammon notes that the grays seemed vulnerable from the very beginning:

> Many of the marked habits of the California Gray are widely different from those of any other species of *balaena*. It makes regular migrations from the hot southern latitudes to beyond the Arctic Circle; and in its passages between the extremes of climate it follows the general trend of an irregular coast so near that it is exposed to attack from the savage tribes inhabiting the sea-shores, who pass much of their time in the canoe and consider the capture of this singular wanderer a feat of the highest distinction. As it approaches the waters of the torrid zone, it presents an opportunity to the civilized

whalemen—at sea, along the shore and in the lagoons—to practice their different modes of strategy, thus hastening the time of its entire annihilation . . . Once captured, however, this whale yields the coveted reward to its enemies, furnishing sustenance for the Esquimaux whaler, from such parts as are of little value to others. The oil extracted from its fatty covering is exchanged with remote tribes for their fur-clad animals, of which the flesh affords the vendors a feast of the choicest food, and the skins form an indispensable article of clothing. The North-west Indians realize the same comparative benefit from the captured animals as do the Esquimaux, and look forward to its periodical passage through their circumscribed fishing grounds as a season of exploits and profit.

The "civilized" whaler, of course, doesn't wait for the seasons of passage for whales to come to him. He goes to the whales.

Captain Scammon wrote that the average gray whale yields 20 barrels of oil, sometimes more. In the mid-1800s, a gallon of whale oil sold at between 58¢ and 79¢. Sperm oil is the spermaceti found only in the sperm whale's case (a reservoir located in the whale's head); it sold for $1.24 to as much as $1.77 per gallon. The value of the take of the entire Yankee fleet came to $10 million in some of those years.

Many of the men who went after the oil-yielding mammals did so as an alternative to remaining on shore unemployed and unfed. When he signed on, a seaman was nominally promised a share in the profits, often calculated at one-sixtieth of the take. The owners of the ships got the larger portion of the profit; the captain got what was considered a fair share. The captain also extracted much, sometimes all, of what the individual seaman might expect to gain by selling, at great profit, tobacco and the clothing the sailor might suddenly need once his initial wardrobe was worn out or destroyed during pursuit of the whales.

Captain Scammon was moved to write:

> We speak of the whaling merchants as being not of that class who anticipated large profits and quick returns, but only a legitimate compensation for their labors, and a fair interest upon the capital invested in the voyages, which required from one to four year's time to accomplish; and often, though

This piece of scrimshaw, from the author's collection, depicts dolphins bow-riding a ship under sail.

the expedition terminated unsuccessfully, the ship was again sent out on another voyage, trusting that continued persever-ance would bring about final success, which in many cases was fully realized.

The Yankee whalers not only provided my family with some un-savory ancestors but they introduced the world to the Nantucket Sleigh Ride—a fast whaleboat trip across the waves fueled by a harpooned whale—and scrimshaw, an American folk art. Scrimshaw, the art of carving scenes on the teeth of slaughtered sperm whales, helped while away the boring hours between strikes while at sea. By the middle of the present century, scrimshaw had become an expensive hobby for collec-tors. (The best known collector was President John F. Kennedy, who was buried with his favorite piece of scrimshaw placed inside his casket.)

Because it deals in dead whale parts, the open sale of scrimshaw is outlawed in many states now, including California. In some places, such as Hawaii, a certificate must prove that the tooth came from a whale killed before the passage of the Marine Mammal Protection Act of 1972. Sales between private collectors continue, of course, but not as a commerce. Nineteenth century scrimshaw has attained the status of historic art, while modern scrimshaw ranges from bad to excellent, depending on the skills of the carver.

The Act also allows for aboriginal take of certain marine mammals, whose ivory can be sold openly if a native American or native Alaskan

The whaling station of the late 1800s at Point Lobos, near Carmel, California (from Capt. Charles M. Scammon).

has first worked it. However, abuses of the law have resulted to satisfy the demand for scrimshawed teeth. Walrus carcasses have been found in the far north with only the tusks removed; the meat and hides, the intended use of "aboriginal take," had been left unused.

California coastal whaling began with the establishment of a station at Monterey in 1851, according to Captain Scammon, or 1854, according to other sources.

The entire Monterey-Carmel area was dotted with whaling companies for about a quarter of a century. Visitors to Point Lobos State Reserve are familiar with Whalers Cove there, where a wooden shanty once used by the whalers still survives. This spot has been described by Captain Scammon:

> The localities of several of the stations are quite picturesque. Some of them are nearly concealed from seaward view, being inside some rocky reef, or behind a jagged point, with its out-

lying rocks, upon which each successive wave dashes its foam, as if forbidding the approach of ship or boat. The one which most interested us is half-hidden in a little nook, on the southern border of the Bay of Carmel, just south of Point Pinos. Scattered around the foot-hills, which come to the water's edge, are the neatly whitewashed cabins of the whalers, nearly all of whom are Portuguese, from the Azores or Western Islands of the Atlantic.

Whaling from shore stations was carried out all along the California coast, from Crescent City in the north to San Diego, and along Baja California at Punta Banda, Santo Tomas and Punta Eugenia. Rhode Island whaling captain J. P. Davenport established a whaling firm in Monterey in 1854 (a small town north of Santa Cruz still bears his name). Captain Davenport was quickly followed by Portuguese whalers who came from the Azores and Cape Verde Islands to seek a livelihood in America. Accustomed to maintaining small farms in their homeland during some seasons and going out to sea the rest of the year, the Portuguese in this country maintained the same pattern, pursuing gray whales from shore in the early spring when the whales traveled north to the Bering Sea. They also hunted humpbacks, then common in Monterey Bay.

Some Portuguese Americanized their names so that their Yankee captains could remember them better; thus Machado became Marshall, or even Clark. California's central coast is still peppered with the names of the Portuguese whalers who settled there: Machado, Pereira, Silveira, Mariano, and old properties along the coast are still referred to by the Portuguese family names they once bore.

By 1880 few whales had survived the onslaught against them along their migration routes and in the lagoons. The survivors began giving the shoreline a wide berth. No longer was it profitable for the merchants and their captains to mount expeditions, and this form of whaling began to wind down, giving the grays the breather they needed to make their first comeback.

The last whale to be taken from shore at Monterey was in 1905. I have particular reason to remember this because in 1969 I interviewed the elderly daughter of that last whaler, who was also the town's marshal. Mike Noon's final victim was a humpback.

CHAPTER FOUR

The Lagoons of Baja California

CAPTAIN SCAMMON WAS NOT TAKEN completely by surprise the day in December of 1857 when his lookout sighted whale spouts amongst the sand dunes. He had already been tipped off by a Mexican he dealt with the previous winter when he had put in to Magdalena Bay, farther to the south. The Mexican had told him of reports from the Baja California Indians that there were lagoons to the north packed, from one end to the other, with whales.

Scammon's momentous sighting was made while he was sailing close to the Baja California peninsula, from which point the land looked like an endless succession of sand dunes. The sharp-eyed lookout who recognized whale spouts for what they were, even though they appeared to come from a sandy expanse, confirmed what Scammon was looking for: the northern lagoons.

At that point the Captain may not have known there was more than one lagoon; he certainly didn't know that Ojo de Liebre Lagoon would go down in history as Scammon's Lagoon. (He later rather matter-of-factly referred to it by his own name!) We can credit him with the discovery of these lagoons from the open sea; we can also credit him with discovering how, by exercising extreme caution, to enter them.

Captain Scammon did not attempt to enter Laguna Ojo de Liebre with his large whaler, the brig *Boston.* He sent for a shallow-draft schooner, the *Marin.* The whaling captains who followed Scammon also used shallow-draft vessels. Some remained outside the lagoons and sent in even smaller whaleboats. Others anchored in the lee of the several islands along the coast and waited for the whales going to or coming from the lagoons, in order to pounce on them in the open sea.

Captain Scammon didn't visit all of the lagoons, but he led the parade. His discovery of the whale nurseries brought a large number of the rest of the Yankee whaling fleet to these waters. Among other lagoons the whalers entered was Ballena (Whale) Lagoon. Guerrero Negro Lagoon got its name from the bark *Black Warrior,* home-ported in Honolulu, which was wrecked there as it was being towed out to open water in December of 1858; it was caught by strong currents and slammed onto shore. Nearby is Manuela Lagoon, named for another whaling ship. The first Yankee to enter this one was Capt. Jared Poole, related to Captain Scammon by marriage. Other seafarers entered San Ignacio Lagoon, the one most frequented by those of us who now follow the whales with more humane intentions.

Captain Scammon describes the violent and bloody encounters in these same lagoons we now visit with loving intentions. In the following account, he explains why both whaler and whale were at greater risk inside the lagoons than in open sea:

> The casualties from coast and kelp whaling are nothing to be compared with the accidents which have been experienced by those engaged in taking the females in the lagoons. Hardly a day passes but there are upsetting or staving of boats, the crews receiving bruises, cuts, and, in many instances, having limbs broken; and repeated accidents have happened in which men have been instantly killed, or received mortal injury.
>
> The reasons of the increased dangers are these: the quick and deviating movements of the animal, its unusual sagacity, and the fact of the sandy bottom being continually stirred by the strong currents, making it difficult to see an object at any considerable depth.
>
> When a whale is "struck" at sea, there is generally but little difficulty in keeping clear. When first irritated by the harpoon, it attempts to escape by "running," or descending to

the depths below, taking out more or less line, the direction of which, and the movements of the boat, indicate the animal's whereabouts.

But in a lagoon, the object of the pursuit is in narrow passages, where frequently there is a swift tide, and the turbid water prevents the whaler from seeing far beneath the boat. Should the chase be made with the current, the fugitive sometimes stops suddenly, and the speed of the boat, together with the influence of the running water, shoots it upon the worried animal when it is dashing its flukes in every direction.

The whales that are chased have with them their young cubs, and the mother, in her efforts to avoid the pursuit of herself and offspring, may momentarily lose sight of her little one. Instantly she will stop and "sweep" around in search, and if the boat comes in contact with her, it is quite sure to be staved.

Another danger is, that in darting the lance at the mother, the young one, in its gambols, will get in the way of the weapon, and receive the wound, instead of the intended victim. In such instances, the parent animal, in her frenzy, will chase the boats, and, overtaking them, will overturn them with her head, or dash them in pieces with a stroke of her ponderous flukes.

Sometimes the calf is fastened instead of the cow. In such instances the mother may have been an old frequenter of the ground, and been before chased, and perhaps have suffered from a previous attack, so that she is far more difficult to capture, staving the boats and escaping after receiving repeated wounds. One instance occurred in Magdalena Lagoon in 1857, where, after several boats had been staved, they being near the beach, the men in those remaining afloat managed to pick up their swimming comrades, and, in the meantime, to run the line to the shore, hauling the calf into as shallow water as would float the dam, she keeping near her troubled young one, giving the gunner a good chance for a shot with his bomb-gun from the beach. A similar instance occurred in Scammon's Lagoon, in 1859.

The testimony of many whaling-masters furnished abundant proof that these whales are possessed of unusual sagacity.

Numerous contests with them have proved that, after the loss of their cherished offspring, the enraged animals have given chase to the boats, which only found security by escaping to shoal water or to shore.

Today we admire Captain Scammon as an early amateur zoologist and for his fascinating eyewitness accounts of the whaling days. When reading his whaling accounts, however, we must keep in mind that he was in fact a whaling skipper and his actions and his thinking must be placed in the context of his time. His was a perfectly honorable profession. He spent eight years at it and because of this, it is remarkable that he could write about whales with concern for the longevity of their species.

While today the death of a whale brings feelings of outrage to most civilized people, in the 1800s whales provided necessary commodities and commerce for entrepreneurs. Charles M. Scammon was born in Maine in 1825 and decided to go to sea when he was 17, not to become a whaler but because he needed a career. After eight years learning the ropes off the East Coast, where he had enjoyed commands of modest ships, Scammon went West to seek greater opportunity. The California Gold Rush was to him such an opportunity, not to prospect for gold but as a way to obtain command of a ship. The Gold Rush fueled a tremendous shipboard commerce in and out of San Francisco and the huge merchant fleet of San Francisco quickly provided him with what he hoped for. He soon commanded merchant ships up and down the Pacific coast and as far away as China.

By 1852 the Gold Rush began to peter out. Merchants looked elsewhere for means of turning a profit. Some ships of commerce were converted into whaling ships, and thus it is that Scammon became a whaling captain.

His writing during those years reveals a compassionate man:

> After evading the civilized whaler and his instruments of destruction, and perhaps while they were suffering from wounds received in their southern haunts, these migratory animals begin their northern journey. The mother, with her young grown to half the size of maturity, but wanting in strength, makes the best of her way along the shores, avoiding the rough sea by passing between or near the rocks and islets

that stud the points and capes. But scarcely have the poor creatures quitted their southern homes before they are surprised by the Indians about the Strait of Juan de Fuca, Vancouver and Queen Charlotte's Islands. Like enemies in ambush, these glide in canoes from island, bluff or bay, rushing upon their prey with whoop or yell, launching their instruments of torture, and like hounds worrying the last life-blood from their vitals.

If the gray whale made it past the coastal Indians of the Northwest, there were the Eskimos to contend with: "The watchful Esquimaux steal upon them, and to their primitive weapons and rude process the whale at last succumbs, and supplies food and substance for its captors." In 1874, long after he had quit the whaling trade and at a time when grays were few, Captain Scammon published his book. In that year he wrote:

> None of the species are so constantly and variously pursued as the one we have endeavored to describe; and the large bays and lagoons, where the animals once congregated, brought forth and nurtured their young, are already nearly deserted. The mammoth bones of the California Gray lie bleaching on the shores of those silvery waters, and are scattered along the broken coasts, from Siberia to the Gulf of California; and ere long it may be questioned whether this mammal will not be numbered among the extinct species of the Pacific.

It seems incredible that whaling captains could be so careless — or greedy — that they gave no thought to the future of the natural resource they so relentlessly pursued. Instead of saving the baby whales, whalers often struck them first, in a deliberate attempt to keep the mother within easy range of harpoons. It didn't take long to empty out the lagoons. In *The Forgotten Peninsula* the late nature writer Joseph Wood Krutch describes that era: "Given hunters so daring, so relentless and so indifferent to everything except the season's catch, it is no wonder that by the 1890s whaling along California's shores ceased because the population had obviously been all but exterminated, and a little later, was assumed to be extinct . . ."

Dr. Krutch then tells of the discovery in 1910 of a "devilfish" being

This baby elephant seal, or weaner, mugs for the camera on a beach on Isla San Benito, off the west coast of Baja California.

Nearly three tons of adult male elephant seal takes a breather at Isla San Benito, off Baja California's west coast.

hunted in the waters off Korea. It turned out to be a gray whale, but of a different stock from the California gray.

> Though the whale being hunted in Korean waters was indeed the same species as that which breeds in Scammon's Lagoon, there seems no reason to believe that there had ever been any interchange between the two groups and a few of the California contingent must have survived because, in the 1930s, after the considerable interval during which they were no longer hunted, both American and Russian ships again pursued them so relentlessly off the California coast that they were again almost wiped out and were saved only by an international agreement of 1938 to protect all members of the species wherever found.

Dr. Krutch observes that one result of this agreement has been the revival of two species endangered in much the same waters by the same hunters: the gray whale and the elephant seal.

The nature voyages I joined to visit the whales at San Ignacio Lagoon usually include stops at the islands off the west coast of Baja California, several of which now function as birthing and mating grounds for elephant and fur seals. The Island of Guadalupe is the main fur seal rookery. At the middle of the three small San Benito Islands, we visited several beaches where the elephant seals haul out during the winter. They are quite unafraid of man and exhibit only mild alarm at close approaches.

On nearby Cedros Island elephant seals and the California sea lions mingle in rare harmony, usually after the male elephant seals have returned to their solitary life at sea. The females and baby elephant seals commune with each other quietly while the sea lions are conspicuous by their barking and cavorting in the surf.

While he never visited the lagoons by land or sea, Dr. Krutch did fly over them and observed the grays in "amorous encounters." These aerial visits occurred in the 1950s, by which time human activity—due to mining of salt flats—had picked up in the vicinity of San Ignacio Lagoon. Erle Stanley Gardner, creator of Perry Mason, also visited the area in the 1950s and made use of both roads and landing strips created to allow the commercial extraction of the salt deposits. Gardner's long love affair with Baja California resulted in his book, *Hunting the Desert*

Whale, published in 1960. In it are the first accounts many of us had heard about the extent of the resurgence of grays in modern times.

Access to these lagoons by road today remains tightly controlled both by the salt company and the Mexican Government and is restricted for casual travelers. The recently-built paved highway that runs the length of Baja California stays far from the whale lagoons. (For this both we and the whales can give thanks.)

The salt industry appears to present no threat to the waters where the grays mate and give birth. Nor do government efforts to establish small farms for the inhabitants using "fossil water" extracted from giant underground reservoirs.

The only possible cloud on the whales' horizon is the persistent rumor that Mexico has found oil deposits in the vicinity of Scammon's and San Ignacio lagoons. Should this be true, tapping these deposits could increase traffic around the lagoons and raise the specter of oil spills and other industrial pollution.

For now, Mexico isn't talking.

The Friendly Whale Syndrome

 THEN I, BEING THEN AT THE HELM and looking on the windward side of the ship, saw a very large whale approaching us.

I called out to the Mate to inform him of it. On his seeing the whale, he instantly gave me an order to put the helm hard up, and steer down towards the boats. I had scarcely time to obey the order, when I heard a loud cry from several voices at once—that the whale was coming a-foul of the ship. Scarcely had the sound of their voices reached my ears when it was followed by a tremendous crash.

The whale had struck the ship with his head, directly under the larboard fore chain at the water's edge, with such force as to shock every man upon his feet. The whale then setting under the ship's bottom came up on the starboard side and directly under the starboard quarter.

Instead of leaving the ship, the monster took a turn off about three hundred yards ahead, then turning short around, came with his utmost speed and again struck the ship a tremendous blow with his head upon the larboard bow, and with such force as to stave in the whole bow at the water's edge. One of the men who was below at the time came running upon deck saying, "The ship is filling with water."

The scene at this moment—no one can ever realize its extent unless they have been in such a situation under similar circumstances . . . Here she now lay, snatched untimely from her stateliness into a mere shadow of what she was and ourselves deprived of the home which her goodly sides had so long afforded us . . .

These lines were written in 1876 by a collateral ancestor of mine, Nantucket whaling Capt. Thomas Nickerson. As a lad of 14 he sailed aboard the whaler *Essex*. One day in the eastern Pacific, some 600 miles or more from the South American coast, a sperm whale, fed up with being a harpoon target, turned flukes—and the tables.

The *Essex* sank on November 20, 1820, and the surviving crew spent three months in whaleboats suffering terrible hardships, eventually resorting to cannibalism. The sinking of the *Essex* provided the climax for Herman Melville's *Moby Dick;* his source was Owen Chase, a first mate who shared the whaleboat with young seaman Nickerson, and who survived to write the account. Chase's account was published in 1821; Captain Nickerson's manuscript did not see print until the Nantucket Historical Association brought it out in 1984. Both men lived to hunt whales again and both received commands.

I suspect that neither captain would believe the events in the lagoons of Baja California 100 years after Captain Nickerson wrote about the hunter becoming the hunted on the high seas!

The first hint of what was in the offing can be found in Erle Stanley Gardner's vivid book about the "desert whale." After retelling the story of the discovery of the lagoons by Captain Scammon, he wrote of the parade of whale ships that followed:

Reading accounts of the hardened whalers of those days it appears that they themselves were indescribably shocked by the slaughter, carried out amidst scenes of confusion and violence, with the desperate whales attacking the whalers, with harpoons and bomb-lances flying, and boats so thick that at

times lines crossed and boats being towed by frenzied harpooned whales crashed into each other.

For a few years this slaughter continued and then suddenly
the gray whales vanished. It was thought they were all extinct.

Gardner further observed: "Nor should one doubt the intelligence of
the gray whale. They soon began to associate the long rowboat, known
in seafaring terminology as the 'whale boat,' with their hunters."

In the years following World War II, scientists took a new interest in
the oceans, Gardner writes. With this interest came the discovery that
the gray whales were once again to be found off the coast of California
and in the Baja California lagoons:

"My friend, Dr. Carl Hubbs, started making aerial surveys to take an
annual census of the whales in the lagoon. And, as reports were made,
the press picked up the information and it soon became known that
whales were returning in numbers to their old breeding grounds."

The late Dr. Hubbs was a pioneer in the modern study of the gray
whale and he paved the way to much of what we now know about them.
Two other of Gardner's friends entered the picture with less vital results. One was Dr. Paul Dudley White, President Eisenhower's heart
doctor, and the other was Donald Douglas of aviation fame. Dr. White
wanted to obtain electrocardiographs from a living whale's heart and
Douglas organized an expedition for him to Scammon's Lagoon. Gardner recalls the first results: "The word 'got around' among the whales
and the expedition came limping back with a stove-in powerboat and
men who had a healthy respect for the whales."

Eventually Dr. White was able to get some lances, appropriately wired
to recording equipment, into a whale by means of a helicopter. The
results were not spectacular but the expedition made news, focusing
more press attention on the gray whales and the lagoons.

It was against this history of "devilfish" and modern instances of
"stove-in boats" that Gardner approached the task of getting close
enough to the whales to photograph them. On his first foray out in a
skiff on Scammon's Lagoon he felt a baby gray whale come up under the
craft and raise it slightly. The boat then slid off the whale's back and
gently into the water. Wrote Gardner: "We got some hurried pictures
but the question always arose, where was Mother?

"In Mother's eyes this was a poor little destitute offspring in need of
attention and protection. To us, he was a seventeen-foot whale still

The enormous head of an adult gray whale, the outline of the mouth showing clearly, emerges beside a skiff at San Ignacio Lagoon.

capable of smashing a boat with his tail or upsetting us in shark-infested waters."

Gardner told of another encounter of the nervous kind that occurred to one of the area residents:

> (Enrique) . . . had taken two men out to paint a buoy, one of the big steel channel markers anchored beside the channel and used to guide ships into Guerrero Negro.
>
> Enrique was sitting in the boat. The two other men, by means of ropes, had climbed up to the top of the buoy.
>
> Suddenly two whales appeared close by. One of them

thrust his head up in order to take a good look, then both of them made for the boat.

Enrique stood his ground.

One of the whales punched the boat with his nose, then the other one came up and nuzzled it. That was too much for Enrique.

He grabbed a rope and scampered up the side of the buoy . . . The two whales hung around and held the men up on that buoy for nearly an hour. They seemed to enjoy having their quarry treed. From time to time they would stand up on their tails in the water to look at the men from a level stance, then they would come down and swim around the buoy, then they would come up and nuzzle the boat. They then would swim off and, like cats playing with a mouse, pretend to be disinterested, only suddenly to return.

Enrique had never seen anything like that happen before in the eleven years he had been around the lagoons.

It was his idea that whales were absolutely and completely unpredictable, that each whale was a law unto himself and that any whale could attack any boat at any time, although he felt certain the majority of whales were inclined to be peaceful.

Peaceful, indeed. Or friendly. The difference between an attack and a nuzzle is the difference between war and peace. Considering the intelligence of cetaceans, and the gray whales' experience with the human race, I don't feel it is unreasonable to believe that these whales either noticed that recent generations of their kind were not being harassed in the eastern Pacific, or else this lack of harassment resulted in the loss of all memory of harassment at the hand of humans.

Whatever, this was the first description of what has come to be known as the friendly whale syndrome.

It was not until 17 years later that the friendly intentions of the gray whales of the Baja California lagoons were verified. The late Dr. Raymond M. Gilmore, for many years associated with the San Diego Natural History Museum, chronicled the phenomenon. Acting as naturalist aboard boats especially chartered to go out and meet the migrating grays off the California coast, he could be considered the father of organized whalewatching. His first such trip was in 1959. The one that made whalewatching history, however, took place in 1976. (This was, by the way, the third year that boats had visited San Ignacio for whalewatching cruises, but it was the first year that friendly activity had been encountered.) His amazing account was published in *Terra*, the magazine of the Natural History Museum Alliance of Los Angeles County, in the summer of 1976:

> **23 February 1976.** Laguna San Ignacio, west coast Baja California, 430 nautical miles south of the California border. Aboard the sportsfisher, *Qualifier–105,* a Natural History Museum Alliance charter with more than thirty passengers aboard.
>
> Over the radio-telephone from a nearby boat, the *Royal Polaris,* John Sloan, leading, talking, came a story I found hard to believe, to wit: A gray whale, female, was persistently playing around the ship and its skiff tied astern.
>
> But it was true, as I learned to my amazement at various times during the next two days.
>
> This very friendly whale would swim back and forth, around and under the larger sportsfishing boats, sometimes scraping the bottom with its back or head. Then it would leave, usually for no apparent reason, and then return in a while to repeat the performance.
>
> Sometimes it would touch, nudge, or bump a skiff that was tied astern. But when people were in the skiff, the friendly whale would present itself alongside and solicit attention, in one case even ignoring an adjacent empty skiff. After recovering from initial shock, the people would reward the whale by rubbing or patting it on the head or back.

This friendly whale (there is always the possibility that it was more than one whale, although Dr. Gilmore thought not) continued contact with a variety of visitors to the lagoon through the following month. The whale's length was estimated to be between 28 and 35 feet; underwater photos revealed that she was a female. While Dr. Gilmore wrote that he himself saw only one whale, other friendly whales in Laguna San Ignacio were reported to him by reliable sources. (Other whales reported included "cows with calf, an immature whale or two, and an unusual pair of 'lightly courting' immatures or sub-adults seen on

February 16th, according to an excellent and detailed description by (whalewatcher) Fran Broomfield."

Attempting to shed some light on the reasons for this friendly behavior, Gilmore noted that "courting pairs and especially trios, and tetrads, common in the lower or outer parts of lagoons, have also been indifferent to the presence of boats, especially if the approach has been quiet." He additionally reported on curious baby whales who would approach boats and rubber rafts before being nudged away by the anxious mother.

The friendly activity, according to Dr. Gilmore, seemed to take place only in San Ignacio. To this date, such activity has been extremely rare in the other major lagoons; as of this writing, I have heard of only one instance in Scammon's Lagoon. Dr. Gilmore theorized that the other lagoons are too large and that boats in them do not congregate together. In Laguna San Ignacio, however, he says that:

> boats and skiffs are concentrated because of the lagoon's small size, in about three square miles. Whales in this lower and navigable area of the lagoon have thus been almost constantly associated with boats and skiffs including Mexican fishing *pangas*. Therefore there could have been a closer and more continued association of boats and whales, to which the whales gradually adjusted in steps, such as:
> 1. indifferent tolerance of ships
> 2. then curious approach
> 3. then voluntary play with inactive rubber boats or skiffs that were tied astern of larger boats, and finally
> 4. active and persistent solicitation of attention from people in small boats by the boldest whales.

At first it was only natural that scientists and naturalists alike would come to the conclusion that the friendly whale was Gigi, a gray whale who had spent a year in captivity and in close association with humans at Sea World in San Diego. But those who knew Gigi were able to state that the star of Sea World had distinctive markings which she would not have outgrown; Gigi was positively identified three years later in 1977 in San Ignacio Lagoon with a baby.

As a baby, Gigi was captured in Scammon's Lagoon on the afternoon of March 13, 1971. A collecting expedition from Sea World, headed by

Gigi is seen days before she was released into the wild, too large for her tank at Sea World in San Diego.

staff veterinarian Dr. David. W. Kenney, had obtained permits for the rare undertaking from both the American and Mexican governments. The little—at 4,000 pounds and 18 feet—gray whale was captured by hoop-net technique, a method used for years to capture pilot whales and, in some instances, dolphins. Sea World stated that this "capture

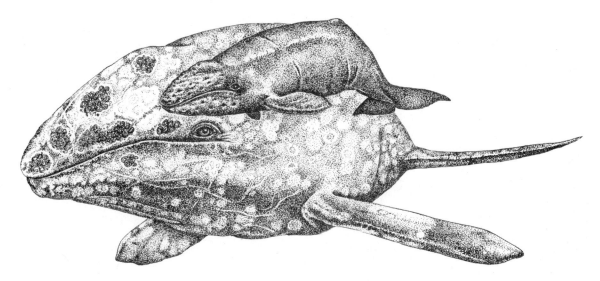

Gray whales

technique fully protect(s) the animal as he dives through the hoop to get away, pulling the net over two-thirds of his body and becoming secured."

Gigi took well to captivity and grew normally in a 55,000 gallon filtered sea water tank. Periodic reports from Sea World became part of a valuable study of the natural history of gray whales. The reports noted that at first "Gigi acted like a human baby, sleeping most of the time. Sea World began tube feeding her with a formula on March 18, 1971 . . . By early June, she had begun picking up squid from the bottom of the tank, and by July 1, was considered completely weaned."

As Gigi grew she required more space; eventually her home at Sea World became Shamu Stadium's 1-million-gallon tank. Scientists from far and wide came to perform a variety of tests on her and she grew used to human company and human attention. A year later, in compliance with terms of her capture, Gigi was released into her natural environment, the open Pacific. On that day, March 13, 1972, she had grown to 27 feet in length and weighed approximately 14,000 pounds.

A lightweight tracking device monitored her migrations for six months. The device lasted long enough to prove that, despite some fears, Gigi took kindly to her release back to nature. Her feeding and migration instincts had remained intact.

Conjecture that the first friendly contact was Gigi was widely reported and the behavior was explained as being the result of a whale accustomed to human contact. But the friendly whale syndrome cannot be credited to Gigi; the phenomenon evolved by itself. That this is so establishes a hopeful new chapter in the story of human contact with whales.

Not the least of this hopeful note is the bond of awareness and concern established between one baby whale and a vast human public.

CHAPTER SIX

The Friendly Encounters Increase

EVER SINCE THAT FIRST FRIENDLY ENCOUNTER in 1976, a parade of scientists, researchers, naturalists and plain ordinary whalewatchers has gone to Baja California. Long before Dr. Gilmore's first reports of the friendly whale syndrome, the Mexican Government had wisely placed controls on access to the lagoons. These controls may well have saved the grays—rescued from harpoons for a second time by international agreements—from being killed by kindness.

The controls placed on human activity in the Baja lagoons have been both farsighted and beneficial. In a decree dated December 6, 1971, the Mexican Government made Scammon's Lagoon a gray whale sanctuary.

With justifiable pride the Mexican Government noted:

> Cabe señalar que esta fué la primera zona de reserva para ballenas en el mundo y recibió el amplio reconocimiento por todos los gobiernos conservacionistas participantes en la comisión internacional ballenera [It is to be pointed out that this was the first whale reserve zone in the world and it received full recognition by all the conservationist governments participating in the international whaling commission].

Esta acción ha permitido que las ballenas se reproduzcan en esta área y el resultado ha sido la recuperación paulatina de estas poblaciones de cetáceos [This action has allowed the whales to reproduce in this area and the result has been the gradual restoration of these cetacean populations].

In 1979 the government broadened the decree to include Laguna Guerrero Negro (Black Warrior Lagoon) and Laguna Manuela. Controls were entended to San Ignacio Lagoon several months later. The controls require those entering the lagoons by boat or by land to obtain a permit from the federal Department of Fisheries. The number of boats and people allowed at any one point at any one time is also spelled out in the regulations.

Mexico's action came before reports of friendly whales; additions were made to the decrees during the ensuing periods of increased human activity. Mexico also formed a marine mammal research group, Investigaciones con Mamíferos Marinos en México, in the mid-1970s and in 1979 the National Program of Research and Conservation, which is concerned with research on whales and their environment. The program's chief is Dr. Luis Fleischer, one of Mexico's most distinguished experts on marine mammals. He is currently an officer of the Technical Committee of the International Whaling Commission and is headquartered with the Fisheries Department in La Paz, Baja California Sur. He has led annual student study groups to the lagoons in recent years.

When I asked him his opinion of the whales' astounding friendly behavior, he gave me a scientist's cautious reply: "The whys still are open questions we must solve." But he ventures, "Perhaps there is a relationship due to the tourist activities developed in San Ignacio Lagoon in the past years . . . Perhaps the whales there were most exposed to boats and human close contact and interaction occurred more frequently.

"Perhaps," he added, "they always were 'curious' about boats but there were not enough 'curious people' to get close? Perhaps the 'friendly' whales are young sexually aroused whales?"

Dr. Fleischer says the friendly behavior first noted in San Ignacio Lagoon has occurred in Scammon's and Black Warrior lagoons only since 1983, and then only with two whales. But he does wonder if perhaps all this closeness may be "an unnecessary and risky great experience. After all, the joy of the 'majesty' of the whales does not decrease with distance!"

An adult approaches a skiff at San Ignacio Lagoon.

The first time I was in a small skiff in San Ignacio Lagoon when a mother gray whale slowly surfaced within inches of us, I must admit that "risky" was one of the words that ran through my mind. As of this writing, however, there has been only one instance of unfriendly behavior on the part of the whales in any of the lagoons. A skiff with at least 10 persons in it approached a baby whale during a whalewatching trip to Scammon's Lagoon in February, 1983. As they closed in on the baby, the mother appeared out of nowhere, came up under the skiff and then struck it with her flukes. One of the whalewatchers, a 60-year-old man from Los Angeles, died of a heart attack soon after. A second man, a 65-year-old professor who was conducting research for a book on whales, was struck on the head by a flying oar and died of his injury a few days later.

Anticipation of such an accident has failed to dampen human ardor for the lagoon experience either before or after this unfortunate incident. Both professional groups and commercial whalewatching parties have visited the lagoons ever since the "word got around," as Erle Stanley Gardner would have put it, of that event in 1976.

The California Academy of Sciences in San Francisco conducted a trip to San Ignacio Lagoon for members in February, 1978. Academy Director George Lindsay wrote in the November–December 1978 issue of that institution's magazine, *Pacific Discovery*, about the trip with the same enthusiasm that Dr. Gilmore had shown two years before:

> We had hardly anchored when the skiffs were lowered and we were off to watch whales. John, who operated our skiff, said, "I hope we find the friendly whales," and a few minutes later one appeared. I was unprepared to see a whale's head beside our skiff, its eye directed toward us. Then its nostrils, with a patch of barnacles at its side, were in my camera viewfinder. I knew what was going to happen but froze with my finger on the shutter release. The whale spouted and we were drenched. My picture is of water spray. It was clean and the breath was without odor.
>
> Other skiffs approached and the "friendly" whale went from one to another, dividing its time between us. When it disappeared for a few minutes everyone watched the water with keen excitement and a little apprehension, but the "friendly" whale did not touch the skiff. Once, when everyone was looking forward, expecting it to appear off the bow, the whale rose dramatically in a spy-hop behind them. David Cavagnaro, in another skiff, saw the expectant observers being observed by the intended object of observation.

Accounts of the increasing number of contacts with the friendly whales accelerated every year. Some were written in breathless tones, others with proper scientific graveness. Some of the old-time researchers were able to embark upon a whole new field of study, while some of the newer graduates established their credentials with their work in the exciting new field offered by contact with the grays in Baja California.

Until recently, just about everything we knew about whales came from the study of corpses, which is akin to learning about human behavior from cadavers. Those studying the physiology of whales did so by carving up bodies tossed onto beaches and already in a state of decay. Much of our early knowledge comes from researchers allowed to accompany the whaling fleets to the Antarctic. But, their mission was of little importance as far as the profit-minded whalers were concerned, and they had to do their research as the flensing knives sliced away. Earlier in this century this practice gave rise to many conflicting conclusions about the life cycle of the whales. For some reason, scientists

A gray whale passes a skiff at San Ignacio Lagoon.

accompanying the Portuguese whalers off Africa had a run on slaughtered female whales bearing twin embryos. This fostered an impression Captain Scammon falsely perpetrated with his drawing of a whale suckling two babies at once. Such a thing is pretty much a physical impossibility; should a whale bear twins, more often than not only one is fed.

Much of what was added to whale natural history until the mid-1970s was knowledge extrapolated from dolphins which, because of their size, have been in seaquaria for more than thirty years now. But now, in the lagoons, researchers and whalewatchers surrounded by friendly whales have an unprecedented opportunity to study the living animal.

Gray whales come to the lagoons one year to mate in the warm and buoyant waters, and they return a year later to bear their young. (The gestation period for a whale is 12 to 13 months.) Observers in the lagoons have confirmed that as often as not, both the act of giving birth and the act of mating are accomplished with the help of a third party. In Hawaii I was accustomed to reports of humpbacks giving birth with a third whale, referred to as an "auntie," standing by. The auntie assisted in getting the baby to the surface for that all-important first breath. (The auntie also was more often male rather than female.) In the Baja California lagoons, researchers have observed a third whale lean against a copulating couple to help keep them close together!

The lagoons have allowed researchers their closest and most frequent looks at the actual birth of a whale. Although migration is timed to get them to the lagoons to give birth, there are births at sea, usually during the final days of a migration. In 1986 a few births were reported farther north. Alan Baldridge of Stanford University's Hopkins Marine Station on the Monterey Peninsula wrote in an American Cetacean Society newsletter (February, 1986), "This expansion of the calving range to include the coastal waters of Central California is a recent phenomenon."

The expectant mother will not put into whatever protected bay is handy when her time is at hand. If the female is about to give birth, she will head for the closest lagoon, not necessarily the one she prefers. For that reason, the first births of the season apparently take place in Guerrero Negro Lagoon, the first of the lagoons the southbound gray encounters. The next lagoon is Scammon's Lagoon, followed by San Ignacio. Thus, the number of babies born early in the season, in December, is greatest at Guerrero Negro. Scammon's is the lagoon where more than half the year's crop of babies is born; California's bays are largely ignored.

The National Marine Fisheries Service quotes Dale W. Rice, one of their researchers, as establishing that 9 percent of the calves are born in Guerrero Negro, 53 percent in Scammon's Lagoon, 11 percent in San Ignacio, and 12 percent in Estero Soledad. Magdalena Bay and a few other minor birthing areas each make up about 6 percent of the total and a very few are born on the other side of Baja California inside the Sea of Cortez.

Once having given birth, according to some researchers, many mother whales will lead their baby to another of the lagoons. No explanation for this behavior has been offered, although it may have something to do with the mother's memory of her own nursery at infancy. San Ignacio Lagoon appears to be a favorite in this respect. It is expansive at 4 by 20 miles wide. Whalewatching boats are allowed only in the first three miles of the lagoon, so the females and their babies are alone during the babies' first few weeks.

As the baby grows older, the mother starts to lead him out of the shallow upper sector into the middle and finally the lower lagoon. The uppermost reaches of the lagoon make it easy for the baby to keep blowholes above water while learning the everyday reality of living. Babies have even been stranded on sand bars and both adult and baby corpses have been found. A stranding is not always fatal; researchers Steven L. Swartz and Mary Lou Jones write that they both saw two instances in a single day when a mother beached herself beside a stranded baby and wiggled and pushed until both were back in the water.

Pity the poor mother gray whale! She gives birth to a baby already a third her own length; although the newborn whale averages 15 feet, it hasn't yet acquired the girth that gives its species its Latin name, *Eschrichtius robustus*. At birth, gray whales can weigh as much as 2,500 pounds, robust for a baby but hardly a match for a grownup gray whale, which can reach 45 feet and weigh at least one ton per foot. (Female grays, it might be noted, tend to outweigh their mates, averaging five or six feet longer.) The mother whale's milk is among the richest, in excess of 50 percent fat. Some young whales put on as much as 100 pounds a day on this diet, notably the humpbacks. Gigi, nurtured on an artificial formula, added about 15 pounds a day. There is conjecture that in the wild this daily poundage increases. The baby does not suck out the mother's milk; the mother shoots it out in large servings when the baby mouths one of the two teats contained in a fold in the mother's body—a neat solution to the problem of lunching while under water!

Having grown to a ton or more, a baby whale has all the fearless curiosity of any youngster. Mother and child linger in San Ignacio well into April, sometimes until the first week of May. By the time the baby has grown enough for the mother to take it into the deeper waters of the lagoon, it is ready for friendly encounters. Childish curiosity may be another reason for friendly whale activity.

The fact that the grays linger so long in the lagoons brings up another long-debated subject: Do whales eat while on migration and at their destination? For a long time, scientists agreed that the grays, along with other migratory whales such as the humpback, ate only in their summer grounds. The cold, rich waters on the three sides of Alaska, these scientists wrote, provided all the food they needed. Whales were noticeably skinnier as they headed back north after a winter in calving and mating grounds, scientists said, and this proved that they lived solely off their blubber for months at a time.

A growing number of researchers now dispute that conclusion. Early findings were based on skimpy personal observations. The advent of what I am tempted to call the "save-the-whale generation" has allowed more firsthand observation of certain whales, especially grays and humpbacks, than at any time before, say, 1970.

Amateur naturalist that I am, I feel I have observed feeding activity among the humpbacks off Maui and have photographed them when their throats were so extended that the only possible thing they could have been doing was gulping in quantities of water filled with small fish. The water I saw streaming from the edges of a whale's mouth had to be the result of the tongue's straining action through baleen, trapping dinner inside.

Observers also report gray whales lingering on deliberate detours from their migration route along the California coast. I've seen them come in almost to the edges of the rocky shore at Point Lobos, apparently searching for something edible. There have been numerous reports of grays "eating" kelp off the Pacific coast. (Actually, they regurgitate the kelp, retaining the critters that are attached to the kelp fronds.) In the lagoons of Baja California there have been reports of grays circling under water, leaving a trail of rising sand in their wake. This, many now agree, is typical gray whale feeding activity: The whale sounds, scoops up a mouthful of sand and filters out bottom-dwelling food, then rises to the surface again for air.

It has also been noted that grays tend to move toward the entrance of a lagoon as the tide goes out. A popular theory is that they do so to feed on the organisms stirred up by the force of the tide. According to Swartz (*Whalewatcher,* Fall 1980), mangrove, which grows along parts of the lagoons, adds large amounts of organic matter to the water, thus supplying "significant amounts of organic material and dissolved nutrients to the marine food chain." He also noted that amphipods, abundant in the lagoons, constitute "the major food source of gray whales."

It now seems safe to assume that grays do not fast during their migrations; on the other hand, they do not appear to eat the huge quantities of food during migration that they do in Alaskan and Arctic waters, thus explaining the weight loss researchers have been noting for years.

Since the advent of the friendly whales, some yachtsmen and fishermen have been rethinking early impressions of contacts with whales. Over the years they have flown into a panic when whales approached their boats. And there were instances when whales sank small boats. Most of the stories I have heard have always started out with the statement, "First, we heard this bump . . ." It appears to me that the boats had somehow made first contact with whales, perhaps sleeping whales. And a startled whale might certainly respond to boats by defending himself. The result of such incidents has often been hysterical reports of "whale attacks."

An adult gray whale gets her barnacles scratched by whale-watchers at San Ignacio Lagoon.

The grays' growing penchant for human contact was explored during the course of a whale symposium held in 1985, sponsored by the Tacoma (Washington) Zoo Society. Speakers noted an increase of grays being sighted closer to land than usual. Moreover, the grays were approaching boats with greater frequency and seeking to rub themselves against hulls. At the symposium it was noted that grays were also showing up close to the shores of Washington and British Columbia and within Puget Sound in increasing numbers. Dr. James Darling, a cetologist based in British Columbia, told the gathering that the whales "frequently cruise shorelines in search of boats that offer a good pat."

Normally, he noted, grays rub themselves on sand bars, but in recent years in Mexican lagoons, they've sought out boats with humans in them.

A continuing concern among both scientists and laypersons is the effect constant contact with humans will have on the grays.

"We don't know what this new behavior means," Darling said, "but not too many wild animals have benefited from such close contact with man.

"While the gray whales are still being hunted, they could wander up to the wrong boat. Can you imagine what it would be like with 17,000 gray whales looking for a boat to rub on?"

Darling reminded everyone present that grays did have a history of turning on boats and smashing them if a human in that boat had hurled a harpoon.

"So, as a warning," Darling said, "if you're out on Puget Sound and one of these gray whales comes up to your boat, let him do whatever he wants!"

CHAPTER SEVEN

The Magic Lagoon

THAT FIRST MORNING INSIDE SAN IGNACIO LAGOON I went up on deck before the sun had risen. My styrofoam cup full of black coffee kept my hands warm. Actually, it wasn't cold out; it just seemed, in the colorless half light, that it should be cold, and probably a little damp, too.

The flat water of the lagoon, the distant gray sand of the shore and the sky all had the same color and feel. The world around me seemed dead. I braced myself for disappointment. The buildup and the expectations had been too much.

Dull clangs and leaden thuds came from the galley behind me. Breakfast was about ready. A few footsteps sounded on the wide fishing deck around me and in the passageways below.

I looked up the ladder that climbed the port bulkhead to the open-air cubicle that passed for crew's quarters. Two seemingly lifeless feet rested on the outer rim of the bridge. I could make out part of the skipper's form, huddled inward but clearly on the alert. I wondered if he ever slept. (I'm sure he did, I just never caught him at it.)

The light increased but the sun had yet to put in an appearance. The world began to take on some color. The gray sand got whiter and the gray water and the sky overhead acquired a hint of blue. A fog bank or mist at the horizon began to separate from the other grays and became a solid and separate form of its own, then ever so slowly started to dissolve.

The evening before we had been briefed with the words, "The gray whale is an exuberant animal. Play is very important to them." I contemplated this idea while the gods gradually raised the lights on the stage that morning. The sun began its climb in earnest, first with a theatrical pink tint, then a light yellow filtered by the mists. Gathering up its full intensity, the sun would soon burn away the mists and bring the world to life.

I must have sat at the rail for almost a half-hour, aware of how still everything was, how silent. Then the gods who turned on the stage lights gave the cue for action.

I recognized the sound perfectly well, but I started and the hair on the back of my neck rose. First came a vibrant stillness followed by an explosive hiss like a giant boiler giving off a massive buildup of steam. Not 50 feet away from me a fully grown gray whale surfaced and exhaled.

All whales sound that way when they come up. I had heard it a million times among the humpback in Hawaii and have heard captive cetaceans do it in seaquariums. But this particular explosion of life had a special promise about it.

People erupted from the galley, from belowdecks, from all sorts of unexpected nooks and crannies of the *Qualifier–105*. Everyone aboard rushed to the rail closest to the whale, causing the ship to list slightly. The gray hovered at the surface, gliding forward effortlessly from the momentum of its thrust to the surface.

Even though we aboard had read everything we could about gray whales, had looked at all the drawings and had marveled at photographs; even though two naturalists with the excursion had briefed us with slides and lectures, nothing could have prepared us for a close encounter with this living breathing animal. The mottled color and the clusters of barnacles in the living flesh had a vibrance that none of the drawings, photos or slides could convey. This creature radiated life.

The flesh was scarred, dented and pocked, just as we are; we could now see, up close, that the gray whale is not entirely gray but rather discolored by giant reverse freckles. And up close the huge clusters of barnacles seemed as though they must be painful.

The whale exhaled again, this time almost like a sigh, and then this

An adult gray whale surfaces near the nature expedition ship **Spirit of Adventure** *at San Ignacio Lagoon.*

magnificent animal glided away from us without haste or fear. He[1] seemed to sink slowly from view. Just as effortlessly, he surfaced again, no farther from the boat but parallel to it. Rolling slightly to one side, a great, unblinking eye stared right at us. He showed no emotion at what he saw; he righted himself and, with a final sigh that produced only a slight puff of mist, he sank from sight again.

Our appetites had been whetted, but not for breakfast. The skipper advised us it would take 10 minutes to get the skiffs and lifejackets ready. We gulped down our breakfast and returned to the rail, where three skiffs, each taking six of us plus a crewman, disembarked.

That first morning a breeze had come up almost with the sun and we now headed into a slight chop. As a precaution, I had my camera protected inside a plastic garbage bag, and held it ready to take a chance photo amid the chop.

---

1. At the risk of being accused of anthropomorphism yet again, I cannot continue to use the customary asexual designation. Nor can I go along with the references to female whales as cows, babies as calves and males as bulls. These bovine terms belie the grace of these elegant mammals.

It is common amongst some of us naturalists to refer to most of the whales, especially the larger ones, as "she," especially if a baby is present. Fully developed whales who are alone are probably male and are therefore referred to as "he." As a "naturalist," rather than a "scientist" or "researcher," I take this liberty without a twinge of conscience.

Afterwards I wrote in my notes:

> Whale spouts are already visible. We come across three
> whales, apparently two males and one female, rolling and
> churning in a single group . . . flippers stick straight up, then
> roll over, an occasional fluke . . . usually one side of the fluke
> comes out of the water, the other part remains submerged,
> then it starts to rotate, indicating that the entire body under
> water is rotating—all three in unison.
>
> They roll over and the 'pink floyd' sticks up out of the water,
> rather limply, eight to 10 feet long . . . One of the naturalists
> says that the whale penis apparently doesn't get completely
> erect, but remains limp enough to search snakelike for the
> female's opening while they both sway about in their undulat-
> ing water world.

Our skiffs fanned out three or four hundred yards apart. Whales surfaced here and there, singly and with babies. At first we seemed to have
no effect on them whatsoever; they took our skiffs as a natural part of
their world.

The childish curiosity of all animal young soon took hold. A baby—
weighing nearly a ton—nosed toward us. The chop caused a slight
splash, but the baby moved with an innate grace that would not have
stirred a ripple had the water been calm. I had noticed in Hawaii that
if we were closer to a baby humpback than we were to the mother,
the mother would quickly glide in a circle to place herself between us
and her offspring. Here not only didn't it matter to the mother that the
baby was closer to us, she seemed to want the baby to find out that we
were harmless.

I looked over to the next skiff a hundred yards away and saw crewman
Kevin leaning out of the boat and vigorously scratching a wide clump
of slate-gray whale. His six passengers watched, frozen motionless, eyes
popping, mouths open in a curious smile.

Our crewman Cliff sidled our skiff over toward Kevin's skiff; Sam, in
the third, did likewise. The mother and baby near us followed us as we
closed in, along with the other skiff, on the two mother grays and their
babies visiting with Kevin. Before long we were surrounded by friendly
whales, while the whales were surrounded by friendly us.

"For the next two hours," I recorded soon after in my notebook, the whales, almost always mothers with babies, repeatedly approached our skiffs, swam under us, hovered under the skiffs, swam toward us at the surface, then submerged just enough to swim under the hull . . . and come up on the other side. They would surface beside the skiffs, sometimes upside down as if to present their chin to be scratched.

Humans rubbed whale heads. Whales would come up to our three skiffs at once and all three skiffs would have whales. Sometimes the skiffs were within yards of each other and the whales would slide from one to the other.

I was not just a little nervous. The one-ton babies were impressive enough, but a 35-ton mother bumping our 16 foot-long skiff unnerved me, no matter how much I love whales! I was especially concerned about my camera. If I hadn't needed the photographs—and about half our group didn't have cameras—I would have relaxed more. The thought of being upset and tossed to the whales didn't bother me a whit. They had already proved themselves to be gentle: It was the camera I was worried about. At one point I reached down to touch a whale, but we were just at the edge of a wave, and as she sank, I rose. Michael Ellis, one of the naturalists, was luckier.

"Look! Whale lice!"

He plucked from the whale's head what, for some strange reason, is called a whale louse. These infestations that seem to swarm as lice are crusteceans that look like tiny crabs. Grays of all ages have them, and researchers say they are passed at birth from the mother's genital slit. Whale lice consume algae and parasites that would otherwise accumulate on the whale. This particular louse, a cyamid, was about an inch long, not quite as wide, and one of three types found on the gray whale. (This louse was later identified as *Cyamus scammoni*, named after Captain Scammon.)

At that moment, however, I wasn't concerned about lice, whale or other kinds. I was rapidly losing my nervousness and, keeping a shutter hand dry, didn't hesitate to dunk the other hand in the water whenever one of these enormous creatures cuddled up to us.

Then they disappeared all at once. In the quiet, the silence left behind, we wondered what had we done to offend them? Then once again we were surrounded. The baby whales especially liked to have their baleen rubbed, obviously glorying in the feel of a human hand firmly rubbing the fledgling baleen. Would the Ph.D.'s buy "baleening" instead of "teething"? Probably not.

At one point I was aware of the pap-pap-pap of the prop to our outboard engine coming out of the water, while the boat moved backwards slowly.

"What?" I asked Cliff.

"Look up ahead. We're being pushed backward!"

Sure enough, ahead of us a full-grown whale pressed her head hard against our bow (there had been not a hint of a jolt). Perhaps the vibration of the outboard gave her a tingle in the head. For a full five minutes she held this position, blocking our forward progress. Then, the 35-foot whale sank from sight. The pap-pap-pap stopped; we moved forward. Behind us, the whale bobbed to the surface and cleared the water from the area around her blowholes with a half-hearted puff. A touch of mist appeared over her head, then quickly faded. A baby romped after her, looking like the mother whale in miniature—if a baby the size of a skiff with seven people in it can be spoken of in terms of miniatures.

Once again, something we couldn't see or hear called the whales and without flurry or fanfare they were gone.

CHAPTER EIGHT

More Friendly Encounters

DURING MY TRIPS TO THE LAGOON, I learned to predict the whalewatching we'd have on a particular day by the weather. On still calm days the whales were relaxed and friendly. On windy days, they seemed preoccupied with the business of breathing, keeping blowholes cleared, and looking above water to see what was going on. Possibly because grays are not deep-divers, they seem preoccupied with what is happening on the surface.

On calm days, the whales would glide along the surface and roll slightly to elevate an eye out of the water. Without pausing, they would take in the view, then roll back on an even keel and maintain a steady pace. On choppy days, they surfaced more often and exhaled, blowing away water caught in the ridge that shields the blowhole. More dramatically, they would spyhop. Standing straight up in the water, slowly and without apparent effort, and manipulating their flukes, they would keep one or both eyes out of the water for a period of time. The entire head would come out of the water, revealing the eye and the outline of the mouth; at other times they would rise up so high that their flippers must have been just below the water's surface. They could hold this position for a minute or longer. When they had seen what they wanted, they would sink back down slowly.

*A baby of nearly two tons —
the twin blowholes atop his
head are visible — emerges to
get a petting from a skiffload
of whalewatchers at San
Ignacio Lagoon.*

On both calm and choppy days the babies occasionally "beached"
themselves atop their mothers for 30 seconds or so. To do this, the baby
would skid out of the water and onto the center of the mother's back,
depending on how much of the mother was submerged. Sometimes the
baby would land resting on top of a fluke. This trick was usually of shorter
duration, since the mother needed to use her flukes for maneuvering.

The smaller babies did this more often. On calm days, the baby seemed
to be cuddling; on windy days, the baby seemed to need to catch his breath.

On one day during which calm alternated with wind, I wrote in my notes:

> We awake surrounded by whales circling, playing, spouting, mating, a couple distant breachings.
>
> The skiff parties get damp. At first the whales are too concerned keeping blowholes cleared, but as the wind dies down they become friendly and visit the skiffs as well as our ship itself. Mostly mothers and babies, amazingly close to the ship. No need to go out in the skiffs with whales coming within yards.
>
> The breeze comes up again. There is much spyhopping. A steady stream of adults spyhop near the boat while the babies get their heads out for a breath of air while skimming ahead.

One of the skiffs returned to the ship, trailing a whale mother and baby behind. A woman boarded, saying as she climbed the ladder, "These whales are friendlier than the last five dates I've had!" I have yet to see a human frown in the presence of whales. They inspire good feelings, along with neverending awe at their size.

Often I found no need to go out in a skiff and risk salt water on my camera lens. Whales often came right up to the ship, leaving the skiffs behind. Even when watching them from the higher elevation of the larger ship, rather than from near water level, the size of the grays makes a lasting impression. If ever I am at a loss for words, it is when wanting to convey the feeling created by something so large radiating so much life.

One day on San Ignacio Lagoon we sighted a full grown gray without tail flukes. The flukes appeared to have been completely severed at the narrowest part of the body, at the base of the tail. Though we were never closer than a half mile of this whale, through my binoculars I could clearly see what I thought was bone. Actually, I am told, what I saw was scar tissue forming a perfect circle where the flukes had been severed from the body. I watched as the whale swam forward and changed direction, through a combination of flipper action and body effort.

On February 14, 1958, Dr. Gilmore recorded sighting a gray whale without flukes near the entrance to San Diego Bay. He later sighted what he concluded was the same whale off Alaska on May 3 and 4. At the rate of 45 to 50 miles a day, he calculated, the whale could have covered that distance. He stated that grays normally swim about 80 miles a day during migration; later studies have shown that they swim up to 100 miles a day at a rate of 4 knots.

A whale could have sustained such an injury in one of two ways: through a collision with a ship or its propeller or through an attack by a pod of killer whales (killer whales often gang up from the rear). Collisions between ships and whales are not common; few whales survive being struck by large ships. The American Cetacean Society published a report in the Fall 1980 issue of *Whalewatcher* that tallied 14 such collisions from 1975 through 1980 in Southern California waters. Collisions were discovered when a whale body was found on shore fatally damaged by being struck, or when ships' captains reported them. In one incident a blue whale was found in Los Angeles Harbor after having been struck by a large oil tanker in the open sea. The body remained at the bow until the ship came to dock. No impact had been felt at the time the 670-foot tanker and the whale collided, but a loss of speed—from 21 to 19 knots—had been noted.

On another trip to Baja California, I encountered another full-grown gray with a different type of deformity. Approaching San Ignacio Lagoon aboard the 86-foot *M/V Spirit of Adventure*, skipper Michael Keating kept a sharp eye out for whales. When he spotted this particular whale, his 25 passengers and the two naturalists knew something different was coming up.

"That guy just doesn't look right," the skipper told naturalists Al Molina and Steve Cooper, pointing to one of a half-dozen spouts about 300 yards ahead of us. With the boat almost in idle, we powered ahead only fast enough to keep us from wallowing in the sea's trough. The grays crossed back and forth in front of us as they made forward progress.

Suddenly Molina exclaimed, "Look at that!" A fully-mature gray whale surfaced ahead. Instead of the usual rolling motion a gray whale uses when surfacing, this entire whale surfaced at once, revealing a tremendous dent about two-thirds of the way back. The whale looked to have been struck hard by the bow of a large boat, hard enough to knock spine and body out of line. His only limitation seemed to be that he could not arch his back to make a normal dive, but he could surface, he could submerge, and he could feed. He was at least 40 feet in length and appeared otherwise to be normally robust.

I asked Molina, a naturalist for the Oceanic Society and a biology instructor at College of Marin (California), if this deformity could be the result of a run-in with a boat.

"It could," he replied, "but it could also be congenital." He paused. "I've never seen anything like it."

I was so sure that the whale's deformity had been the result of a collision that I wanted to report it as such. Fortunately, Molina, the professional, was able to save me from jumping to such an unscientific conclusion.

I recalled the flukeless whale and wondered how both these whales negotiated the entrance to the lagoon; where—and how—they had been hurt; and how they were able to survive despite their handicaps. I am curious to know whether either of these whales are observed by later naturalists.

As my time with the grays in San Ignacio Lagoon went on, my enthusiasm failed to diminish. Only my moods changed. Here are notes I made at the end of a day during a trip to Baja California on the *Spirit of Adventure:*

Day 6: Not as windy in the morning, but slightly overcast, the sun breaking through from time to time. I went out with my camera loaded with black and white film, hoping to better last year's photos for the book. A slow start, but after about a half-hour a mother with a baby probably at least a month old and approaching 20 feet in length started to play with us.

Our crew knows that the passengers want to say they've touched a whale, so all three skiffs (with six passengers each) were immediately within a few feet of each other. Great for touching whales, but too close for good photography. We manage to tear ourselves away from time to time and I did get a few shots that I feel will be what I'm after.

When I can't take photos, I concentrate on the presence of the whales. Last year I experienced considerable nervousness at being within inches of these great—and wild—whales. For some reason, this year I am not nervous at all. But both the mother and the baby were large—she was close to 40 feet and 35 tons, and the baby had been growing for more than a month. They passed directly beneath us a number of times, so close to the surface we could clearly see the barnacles and splotches on their skin through the water. At least twice our skiff touched the mother's back enough so that she moved our skiff to one side, or forward. Several times we felt gentle

An adult gray whale
surfacing beside a skiff
shows the three grooves that
start under her chin and run
down her stomach.

bumps as the skiff and the body of one of the whales con-
nected in passing so close we could reach down under water
and touch them. I must admit it was a strange experience to
see the whale's head go under the boat and see it appear on
the other side, while the flukes still approached us from the
original side. Our skiff was 16 feet in length and less than half
that in beam; we were smaller than the wild baby whale we
were communing with!

The baby acted like any youngster would and bounced
around as the mood moved him, while the mother always
seemed in complete control of both herself and us. Five or six
times during the enounter she either turned or rolled on her

side so that the flukes turned up and out of the water within a foot or two of us. We did not try to touch the flukes, as we had the head or back, because we were not certain how she would react. Both whales appeared to enjoy having their heads and jaws rubbed; the baby especially savored having his baleen rubbed. Several of our group pushed a hand inside his mouth and gave a quick rub the entire length of one side of the baleen and back.

The only thing that gave me anything close to an anxious thought was the proximity of those great flukes—at least 12 feet across and so close to us the mother doubled sideways to avoid hitting us. As always, the mother decided when the encounter was over. She turned as if on signal, with the baby at her side. They swam away at a purposeful pace, she with grace and the baby with a childish bounce. The mother spouted large and wet from time to time while the baby spouted short, childish puffs, looking more as though he were playing games than breathing for life.

We wondered why we were able to make these friendly contacts with the whales. No matter how many theories we came up with, a sense of wonder remained. One night aboard ship I asked naturalist Molina to share his thoughts on the subject.

"The whales initiate the contact," he said. "All we can do is put ourselves in a situation where they *can* initiate the contact. They come to the boat because we provide a diversion.

"There is a maturation: the babies have a lot to learn about being whales. They spend a good part of the end of their stay in the lagoon in the tidal current, which is a sort of bivouac area toward the entrance.

"We are graced by their presence. They initiate whatever happens . . . We are at the disposal of the whales. When the time comes to break off the encounter, it is the whales who end it."

Molina went a step further: "It's interesting to ask, what's in it for the people? Why are they willing to lay out $1,500 to come down here? There's been an evolution on both sides.

"It's an emotional outlet, certainly. Perhaps (people) have watched someone do this on (educational TV) and decide they want to participate themselves . . . to be with an organism that has a mind, a memory, perhaps emotions like us, as opposed to a fish or a snake. That's part of it."

The Why of It

WHY ARE THE CALIFORNIA GRAY WHALES FRIENDLY? We have already read the initial impressions and suppositions of those who first stumbled onto the activity in the mid-1970s. With more than a decade of experience behind us now, the reasons for the phenomenon have come more clearly into focus.

Each evening aboard the ships that make the nature cruises to Baja California, the assigned naturalists gave lectures, explaining what we had seen during the day and preparing us for the next day. Marc Webber, one of the two naturalists aboard Qualifier-105, had degrees in biology and was affiliated with California Academy of Science; his special expertise was in marine mammals. The other naturalist, Michael Ellis, had an M.S. in biology and was what I would call a freelance naturalist; he combined a general interest in marine mammals with passions for botany, ornithology and astronomy—after all, the heavens are the birds' natural habitat.

I asked Marc and Michael how they would explain the friendly whale syndrome.

Michael Ellis said, "The theory is that the sound of the skiffs' outboard motor is on the same wave length as the sounds the whales themselves make. I don't think that sound is saying anything to them. It's not whale talk. But it does get their attention and they come over to see where it comes from."

Marc Webber went into more detail: "I don't think it's just because the outboard motor sound is in their frequency range any more. I think the outboard is a signal and they want to interact with people . . . whatever they think we are.

"At first, it might have been curiosity. But now they know we are there. They can see us. They don't just linger out of curiosity—they come up to us because they want to interact with us. They don't come up to the big boat because they are curious about the boat, otherwise they wouldn't peel off the minute we put a skiff in the water and come up to us and let us touch them.

"They want to interact with us. That's not a very scientific explanation, but that's what I believe."

I also put the question to the experts at the National Marine Mammal Laboratory in Seattle, Washington, operated by the U.S. Department of Commerce's National Marine Fisheries Service. Dr. Howard Braham, the laboratory's distinguished director, had Marilyn Dahlheim, a member of his staff, write out an answer for me. She has spent several years in research of the gray whales both along the Pacific Coast and in the lagoons. She writes:

> The most accepted explanation, to date, is that gray whales are initially attracted to both skiffs and large vessels, due primarily to the underwater noise generated by their engines and/or in the case of large vessels, by their underwater machinery noise (e.g., generators, pumps, etc.). The frequencies emitted by these man-made sources occur at the same frequencies where gray whales produce their sounds.
>
> However, once contact is made between whale and the boat, other factors may come into play. For example, the actual sensation of touch, etc. At this time, we are not sure. Typically, gray whales lose interest in the vessel when the engines are completely stopped. This information suggests that noise is a key factor in maintaining curious whales.

Ending a visit to San Ignacio brings on episodes of the "just-one-more" syndrome: one more day, or at least, one more encounter. As the boat heads westerly toward the shifting entrance, the lagoon seems to be more populated than usual with whales. We see more whales upon departure, of course, because we all use the same access. I hoped to see a whale making an actual exit. I was never granted this wish, and I have found no references to anyone doing so. The whales have navigational instincts humans do not. I assume they know when the water in the channels is at its deepest; their built-in radar must tell them when an obstructing sand bar appears; and they must be able to judge that it is safe to barge through shallows. (Baleen whales like the grays cannot echolocate, but toothed whales can.)

Our boat's pilot used eyes and echolocation. As we neared the estuary we saw a number of spyhopping grays. I couldn't tell if they were looking for the exit or whether they were intrigued by our engines and wanted to see what and where we were. Meanwhile, our crewmen scouted a few hundred feet ahead of us in a skiff.

Outside the lagoon, more grays traveled in singles, with some in groups of three and four. Perhaps they were mothers with their youngsters, getting ready to head north. (I have never detected nor have I read anything indicating that fatherly behavior on the part of a whale exists. I doubt that there is any such bond. Some natural concern between groups of whales and even single whales, one toward another, reaches its peak when a second adult is present to assist at the time of mating or of giving birth. This concern seems to transcend instinctive behavior.) We whalewatchers turned south to seek further adventure, and the grays headed north, parading in an established order: First to leave the lagoons are the newly impregnated females, followed by adult males, then immature females; immature males are usually next in line, and last the mothers and their newborn. Swimming closer to shore now than when they came south, at times they travel right through kelp beds and surf. Along the way humans take up their watch stations to view the spring parade north, just as in winter they watched the grays head south. The whales return to the Aleutians, finding the Unimak Pass and entering the Bering Sea. As the winter ice pack recedes, they forage even farther north in seas that churn with swarms of the minute organisms that nourish them to whale size.

Meanwhile, aboard ship, we head out to more open sea for our southbound journey. At this point, the Baja California peninsula is indented, with the next point of land we were headed for sticking elbowlike out into the Pacific. Below this elbow are the assorted small islands and sand bars that form the western walls of Magdalena Bay. On this run to

The captain stopped the ship off Baja California while we fished for our dinner.

Isla Magdalena, the skipper brought the ship to a complete halt, and we bobbed in silence.

Volunteers accepted poles from the crewmen and we sought nourishment from the sea. Hooks were baited with the little anchovy kept in the deck tanks, and we soon hauled in whitefish left and right while the crew took them off our hooks and tossed them into a holding tank. Sometimes one of us caught a sandbass; the crew tossed these back. Once a line snagged a lobster pot. A crew member brought it to the surface. The pot contained three spiny lobster, one about two pounds, the other two about a pound and a half. Traps, lobster and bait were returned when we left.

After an hour's fishing, the 50 gallon tank was almost full of fish weighing four to five pounds each. Our young cook looked pleased with the catch. When I asked him if he'd remembered to bring the tartar sauce—which is the only reason I eat fish—he snorted, "I make my own!"

We got underway again, heading in a more southerly direction with the sea this time, losing the slight chop we had experienced before on the dog-leg run. Within a half hour we had company. "The lads before the wind," Herman Melville called them—giving dolphin trainer Karen Pryor a great title for the book she wrote about her experiences. The common dolphin, slightly brownish and with a crisscross hourglass design on either side, travels in groups of 50 and more. They charged out of nowhere, appearing to overtake us. Then, after romping around us and back and forth across the wake a half-dozen times, they bounced away as if they found something different to investigate—perhaps a shoal of their favorite food, squid.

Dolphins create the illusion of great speed, but estimates are that they peak at 25 miles per hour. Different dolphins attain different top speeds; some experiments in which Mrs. Pryor took part showed that bottlenose dolphins reach half that peak speed.

Even though the dolphins' speed is mostly illusion, what a delightful illusion it is! Karen Pryor writes that " . . . a school of porpoises never overtakes a ship from the rear. They come in at a tangent, intercepting the ship before it gets to them, and catching their free ride until the ship has gone farther than they wish to go."

The dolphins joining us, then, were stealing a ride from the dynamics created by our ship as it churned through the water. I was surprised to learn that they also ride along with us after dark. One night the skipper turned our lights on, illuminating the ship's bow. Dolphins surfed in the bow wake, taking on a mysterious, otherworldly and utterly fascinating appearance as the water in which they swam—and they themselves—were outlined in luminescence.

This afterdark phenomenon is familiar to most who have been at sea. Also referred to as phosphorescence, the sea water emits a light composed of hazy sparks and lines that look like seagoing fireflies. Phosphorescence is the seafarer's term for bioluminescence. As *bio* implies, living organisms are involved in this phenomenon. Millions of animals tinier than grains of salt live at various depths of the ocean and have the capability of emitting light. Biologists believe this ability serves both to lure prey and to frighten predators. In warmer waters, such as

Common dolphins frolic beside the ship.

we plied off Baja California, as well as deeper into the tropics, these miniscule animals live among the plankton in the ocean's top layers. A disturbance such as the passage of a boat stimulates their glow.

Dolphins rose and sank in perfect rhythm with the flow of the cascading waves washing away from the ship's bow. They fell into darkness then reappeared with the next wave, like neon beings dancing in blackness. We saw them roll over nearly onto their side to look up at us. The smile never left their face, and a haunting presence lingered, as if we were seeing the ghosts of all these creatures. When they tired of us, they simply disappeared, leaving a brief trail of phosphorescent dashes that faded into darkness.

The next day we came upon bottlenose dolphins, larger than the common dolphins we usually encountered. Naturalist Webber told us that the Pacific bottlenose is larger and darker in color than the Atlantic bottlenose, most often seen performing in oceanariums. (Flipper was an Atlantic bottlenose.) Pacific bottlenose dolphins can attain weights of 800 pounds, he said, and can reach 10 feet in length.

"The Atlantic bottlenose is the white rat of whales and dolphins," Marc told us. "We know more about them because they are so easy to get. And much of what we know about whales has been extrapolated from Atlantic bottlenose dolphins."

While he talked, we watched a striped marlin keep ahead of our bow by but a few inches, just barely under water. It was as if we were chasing him and he couldn't get away. After about a minute he disappeared. A lone California sea lion appeared, slowly swimming north, snapping

The beguiling dolphin smile is especially prominent on the bottlenose dolphin.

his head up and looking at us as if he didn't quite believe we were there. I don't know why I am surprised to see a sea lion at sea—perhaps because I'm accustomed to seeing them in groups on the Monterey breakwater and the rocks off Point Lobos. I think of them as family-oriented beings and when I see them alone, I wonder if they are lost or, perhaps, outcasts.

As we voyaged farther south, both the seas and the skies became more heavily populated. Gulls appeared time and again, and now frigate birds were seen overhead, usually singly. (Michael Ellis admonished that all gulls are associated with the sea and that there is no such bird as a "sea gull.") There are, however, Western gulls, Heerman's gulls and ring-billed gulls, he pointed out. Brown pelicans, once endangered because DDT residue made their egg shells so fragile they couldn't last the incubation period, also put in an appearance. As the ship came to a halt briefly outside Magdalena Bay, a brown pelican plopped awkwardly onto the water and bobbed with the waves for a while, looking expectantly at us, drawing nearer and nearer, almost within arm's reach. We had no fish to spare, if that is what he expected from us.

If the dolphins of the night before had seemed haunted in their

A pelican comes up to within a few feet of our ship while we fish in the Pacific off the west coast of Baja California. He thinks we will have something for him to eat.

phosphorescence, then so did the Baja California landscape in the glare of full daylight. Landmarks such as Cabo San Lázaro, Punta Entrada and Isla Santa Margarita appeared to form an uneven, broken and colorless wall, the outer wall of what the charts called Magdalena Bay. This background was ghostly and fascinating. The low walls beyond the bay, rugged, with an occasional splash of green suggesting an oasis, invited closer scrutiny. Bumps and hills of shalelike rock mingled with reddish-brown soil. Far on the horizon, the purple haze that obscured dust storms or soaring ridges deepened the air of mystery that hung over the land we followed, 10 to 12 miles out to sea, on our way to the tip of the peninsula. On the charts the peninsula's tip is called Cabo San Lucas; it recedes slightly for about 40 miles before the other side of Baja California begins and the waters become known as the Sea of Cortez.

Because we did not have a permit from the Mexican Government to enter Magdalena Bay, we moved on south at a moderate speed, averaging 12 to 20 miles offshore, and observed what we could of life in the open Pacific. In the fading midafternoon light, we got a taste of things to come in the Sea of Cortez. A high spout announced a whale, a higher

spout than I had seen before. While the water didn't churn, an obvious movement just below the surface indicated something exciting was about to happen.

Then a large platform of a head appeared, not high out of the water, but enough to reveal the largest whale I had ever seen. The whale's body surfaced, not in a rush of water but gradually, rising rigidly without the arch I was familiar with in watching humpbacks and grays.

Even before the naturalists could verify it, the steel gray color of the body told me that this was a blue whale, the largest mammal ever to inhabit the planet. The whale rose up and settled back beneath the water in one effortless movement, an awesome overture to our visit to the Sea of Cortez.

CHAPTER TEN

The Sea of Cortez

WE ROUNDED THE TIP OF CABO SAN LUCAS in the dark hours shortly after midnight. I slept through it in my tiny, two-bunk cabin so deep into the center of the ship that I couldn't even hear the engines. Only the vibration of the vessel pushing through the water told me that we were in motion.

At 5:30 A.M., a time when night starts to fade into reluctant light, the voice of a naturalist punched through my drowsiness: "We have humpbacks!"

Like a sailor blindly following orders, I fell out of the bunk and pounded heavily up the narrow ladder to a port. I saw only flat, color-less sea. Others joined me, while more eager souls dashed by, up to the deck. In a moment they returned at a slower pace.

"He said it *looked* like humpbacks!" one of them muttered.

I went back to get hot black coffee in a styrofoam cup, my automatic ritual. Coffee in hand, I went out on deck and looked for an isolated spot. For me, this was to be a special day: We were on the point of enter-ing the fabled Sea of Cortez, and I wanted to do it all by myself.

We cruised at a languid pace along the slanting tip of the Baja Cali-fornia peninsula, eastward and slightly north, about a quarter of a mile offshore, still in the Pacific. A high bluff disentangled itself from the monotony of the gray shoreline. As we closed in, more shapes appeared. The bluff hovered over a small open-ended bay. At this point a long stretch of gray beach commenced its eastward spread. The bay, the bluff—the easternmost point on the peninsula—and the hills behind them were called Los Frailes, the Friars.

We anchored 300 yards offshore. On the beach was a Baja California fishing village like many we had come to expect in unexpected places—unexpected because we wondered how such villages managed to sustain any sort of life.

The 12 to 14 houses here looked like large packing crates. As we had seen earlier in the San Benito Islands off the northern portion of the peninsula, no matter how humble their homes, their inhabitants always had well-cared-for skiffs propelled by large outboards of good quality. These were provided as part of the Mexican government's program to expand the capability of small fisherman to provide food for general consumption and to enjoy a livelihood.

A van, two station wagons and a camper, with tarps propped up like awnings to provide shelter from the heat of the sun, cast their shadows over aluminum and plastic recliners. These Americans, here to get away from it all, must have been thrilled to see us drop anchor and skiffs. I elected to stay aboard, while the rest of the passengers and crew swarmed ashore. (My fellow passengers were a highly disciplined group: The moment they hit the sand, they squatted like expectant school children to await their safety lecture and snorkeling session.)

I took up my binoculars and scanned the rest of the beach. Beyond the simple fishing village were new concrete structures with connecting archways, which turned out to be a sportfishing resort under development. A landing strip was just beyond the steep dunes and shale.

A compact Tahiti ketch with San Francisco painted on her side to proclaim her hailing port anchored off shore between the village and the resort-to-be. She sported a self-steering vane; the cockpit fenced with waist-high canvas indicated a ship intended for long-distance voyaging. She looked happy and smug in her isolation, until a tupperware sloop powered in and dropped anchor close by ("tupperware" is a derogatory term used to describe fiberglass sailboats).

For a place that on first glance appeared isolated, there was an amazing parade of life. Two beach buggies bounded from nowhere, each loaded down with several adults and kids. They consolidated at

A jaunty Tahiti ketch (left) and a tupperware sloop share the isolation of Los Frailes, at the tip of Baja California.

one end of the beach, and the gringo adults sat together and chatted while the kids skinnydipped or snorkeled.

One of my fellow passengers, chomping at the bit for some unnautical activity, had gone ashore in jogging shorts. When I looked through my glasses at the forms of human life on the beach, one was missing from among our group. A closer look down the beach revealed a solitary figure pounding ahead on the sand for all he was worth. Not the magnificent departure from San Diego, not the majesty of the whales of San Ignacio, not the nearly religious experience of watching the largest creature ever to inhabit the earth—that first blue whale—had prevailed over the jogger's urge. Here amidst the awesome newness of

Pelicans fly low over the Sea of Cortez; the Baja California coast in the background looks like a slice of the Grand Canyon.

the Baja California peninsula, an otherwise very practical grocer of Chinese extraction had only one thing on his mind the first time he could get his Reeboks on terra firma: to jog! On and on he went until he disappeared from view, later reappearing just as we were about to haul anchor, panting and sweating euphorically. On the days we did not put ashore, the early-morning jogger continued aboard ship—around and around the upper deck, the underside of which was the ceiling of the living quarters below. Shipboard naturalist Ellis even included the following in his log later sent to all of us: "We continue south and I go below to catch some shut eye. But what do I hear? The sound of feet pattering over my bunk: once every 45 seconds." Secretly though, I admired the jogger, because I knew I would have been able to enjoy more of the expedition had I had his stamina!

My own euphoria was getting into high gear as we hauled anchor from Los Frailes Bay, leaving the expatriates to their own peace. We pointed the boat into a path of light laid down on the water by the sun, now nearing its noontime position. The tingling I experienced up and down my neck was a combination of anticipation at finally entering the Sea of Cortez and a feeling strangely akin to returning to a place I had, a long time ago, known and loved. But I had never been to the Sea of Cortez. At this moment I remembered that Baja California is a displaced portion of Sonora, the Mexican state immediately south of Arizona. In the late 1950s, when I worked and studied in Tucson, I took a few days whenever I could put together the time and the money to travel south of the border to Hermosillo and Guaymas.

Guaymas especially was an enchanted place, at least back then. Outside the town, Bocochibampo Bay offered an old Colonial-style hotel, alongside a couple plainer ones, low key and practical. Here the Sonora Desert came down to the seashore in the most amazing fashion. No fields or planted crops or soil sustained the workings of man; just bleak desert meeting a shoreline of sand, boulders and expanses of moonlike surface with clumps of cactus here and there.

Bleak it was, in a way, but at the same time it vibrated with a mystical life of its own.

The Baja California peninsula and Sonoran mainland had long ago been one. The fact that a sea split it down the center did not erase the similarities. While Baja California itself was new to me, it was an extension of a place I had already known. Thus that strange feeling of returning to a place I had once known well and loved.

Geologists tell us that at one time this entire area, from mid-Mexico deep into the American West, consisted of tropical forests and swamps populated by dinosaurs up to 50 feet in length. (Today miniatures of these early reptiles remain in the form of lowly lizards like chuckawallas, geckos, gila monsters and chameleons.) The buttes and the cordilleras that remain, dry and stark as desert-bleached skeletons, are left over from eons of constant beatings from primeval tropical downpours.

The earth here, as elsewhere, heaved, expanded, sank and broke into giant plates. Geologists have dubbed the two plates most important to Baja California and the Sea of Cortez the Pacific Plate, which constitutes all the land west of the San Andreas Fault, and the North American Plate. They continue to rise and fall, grating together. The most important period of activity took place either 20 million or 25 million years ago, depending upon your geologist of preference. About 6 million years ago, the crack between the plates, which we now call the San Andreas Fault, opened up wide and Baja California was born.

The peninsula split off from mainland Mexico, creating a deep crack—two miles in some places today—that kept widening. It continues to widen at the rate of an inch a year. At the time of that early widening, the sea rushed in to fill the gap, creating the Sea of Cortez, or, less romantically, the Gulf of California. It's the world's newest sea.

During the time the San Andreas Fault opened up to form this sea, an age of volcanic activity returned to the area, causing a number of freestanding cones to build up. The Sierra de la Giganta, which runs north of La Paz to the center of the peninsula, was also created then. Volcanic activity continues into historic times. Volcán las Tres Vírgenes, located between Santa Rosalía and the town of San Ignacio, last erupted in 1746, and was reported steaming as recently as 1857. Many of Mexico's earthquakes continue to originate in the ocean off its west coast and in the Sea of Cortez.

The land where La Paz is now located was once in a position between Acapulco and Puerto Vallarta, some distance to the south and east. About 10 million years from now, Los Angeles will have moved, along with the land below it which includes Baja California, to a position where San Francisco is today.

And in 40 million years, Baja California and American California— the old Alta California—will be an island off British Columbia, headed for Alaska.

Truth be known, I prefer things the way they are now.

CHAPTER ELEVEN

Sea of Surprises

"THE VERY AIR HERE IS MIRACULOUS, and the outlines of reality change with the moment. The sky sucks up the land and disgorges it. A dream hangs over the whole region, a brooding kind of hallucination."

A voyage into the Sea of Cortez made this impression on John Steinbeck. In *Log from the Sea of Cortez* he records the lack of monotony in this desert land. The sky plays tricks on the eyes and on the mind, depending on the time of day, the slant of the sun, the shape of the clouds or a lack of them. The sea reflects the weather, and its changes are familiar to anyone who has sailed a ship or walked along a salty shore.

In the Sea of Cortez the light also plays tricks with the land. As we enter the Sea of Cortez, the sea itself is about 100 miles wide. Farther north, toward California, it narrows to some 40 miles before ending at the Colorado River in swamps and moving sand bars. It then swerves away to the west from the river into a couple low lagoons before petering out.

As we cruised along the southern portion of Baja California's eastern shore, the sea itself appeared to be boundless. The land on our port side was alternately a dirty white and a reddish brown; only cactus and dull-green shrubs survived here. Inland abrupt peaks and ridges piled

The sun works its magic on the Baja California shoreline at the Sea of Cortez.

up in successive ranks. Some cliffs dropped down to the sea in wide rock slides, with slabs of shale and large boulders scattered down the sides.

Just as the land managed to give an impression of being alive, the sea burst with life. Living things leaped from the sea and returned to it, swam just under the surface of it, swarmed in it and fed in it or were fed upon. "It is probable that no animal tissue ever decays in this water," wrote Steinbeck. "The furious appetites which abound would make it unlikely that a dead animal, or even a hurt animal, should last more than a few moments."

Early into the Sea of Cortez we saw giant manta rays leaping high into the air and splashing back into the water, looking mysterious and threatening. Though they are cousins to sharks, they are not as sinister. Sailors have also called them devilfish, just as they named the wounded mother gray whale protecting her young. Unlike sharks, which more frequently appear alone, manta rays travel in schools.

Square in shape, these strange creatures have a tail I would swear ends with an arrow, giving the designation "devilfish" a peculiar aptness. They have no flukes but can be considered one large fluke that undulates in waves; thus they propel themselves forward. Two small pectoral fins, unnoticeable to the casual glance, are also used for propulsion. The rays looked clumsy when they hurled themselves out of the sea, but sometimes they flew just under the water's surface ahead of the ship, or more often just off to the side, with amazing speed, two wing tips sticking above water like small shark fins.

The manta rays are one of the unforgettable and surprising sights of the Sea of Cortez. We never had any warning that they were there. They would suddenly leap out of the water, several at time, in a series of slapping motions that sounded like a fat boy's bellywhopper, before falling back to the sea. (One theory for the slapping motion is that the rays are attempting to shake off parasites.)

Although to me the ray is a repulsive fish in appearance, I hear that some species make a very creditable substitute for scallops when cut with a small round cookie cutter and properly sautéed. The manta ray is not among the fish used in this way.

Our first day into the Sea of Cortez ended with an approach to Isla Cerralvo, the first of a line of small islands of various shapes and sizes that range northward along Baja California's eastern coast. Isla Cerralvo—the southernmost of a series of peaks which are either the remnants of the original action of the San Andreas Fault or newer tips of seismic or volcanic origin—is now uninhabited by humans, except for the occasional fishing party.

These islands now host large families of sea lions and vast flocks of birds. Ninety percent of the Heermann's gulls and 95 percent of the elegant terns of the world are said to home in on Isla Raza—about a third of a mile in size—at breeding time every year. The islands also form channels of rich waters, paralleling the Baja California peninsula, that funnel the travels of the great whales. Canal de las Ballenas (Channel of the Whales) is between Baja California's east coast and Isla Ángel de la Guarda; it is the best place to see blue whales, fin whales and Bryde's whales. Whales and dolphins love these waters, which act as a natural fish trap and a home to all sorts of nutrients. The Sea of Cortez supports 650 different species of fishes year round and more in winter.

We dropped anchor in the late afternoon off what looked like a desert island where a few hardy cactus refused to give up. Isla Cerralvo is located roughly 8 miles off the coastline, not far from La Paz, the city of 40,000 that is the capital of Baja California Sur, the state occupying the lower half of the peninsula. (Although we would be visiting La Paz later, we were spared civilization for a few more days.) It is one of the few islands in the Sea of Cortez with a natural water supply that could sustain a small permanent human population. Sixteen miles by four, it has no fulltime inhabitants now. When the padres and the Spanish troops arrived here in the sixteenth century, Indians called the Guia-curas resided here. These Indians didn't like the idea of foreigners occupying their land; they took offense at the attempted establishment of the mission at La Paz and attacked it in 1721, almost before the adobe had dried.

The conquistadores retaliated by landing on Cerralvo, but the Indians hid from them and many of them subsequently moved off elsewhere. Those who remained battled the Spaniards in 1734 and were totally annihilated.

No one has taken up residence on Cerralvo since except the odd itinerant fisherman or diver for pearls. Fishermen still come and go today, but pearl divers no longer come to this region once famed by conquering Spaniards for its black pearls. In the 1940s a disease that has yet to be identified killed off the pearl-bearing oysters; they have not returned.

We made no attempt to go ashore. A few flying fish skimmed the water beside us, none high enough to land on deck, as they often do after dark when they are attracted by deck lights. Some of our group dropped hook and line over the side. Two anglers landed puffer fish that had inflated by the time they were pulled to the surface. These were gingerly plopped into shallow fish tanks where we could watch them floating warily, listing to one side. Their huge eyes followed us as we walked by, their sharp spines poised, almost as if they might shoot out at us.

Dusk fell and, our ship awash in light, swarms of pink or dark red worms came close. These pelagic creatures are part of the fantastic chain in the feeding cycle of the Sea of Cortez. (Later, traveling north, we came upon large patches of red and pink krill floating atop the water.) The Spaniards gave these waters the name Vermillion Sea because of the many swarming creatures of this color. The name that stuck, however, was given by Hernán Cortés' sailing captain, Francisco de Ulloa. He discovered the body of water while on a voyage of exploration for Cortés and named it for his commander. Though properly spelled *Cortés,* decades of gringo visitors pronouncing the *s* like a *z* have brought about a permanent change in the literature.

Frigate birds circle over the pinnacles of Los Islotes de Partida, in the Sea of Cortez.

During the night we traveled some miles farther north and awoke for breakfast inside a tiny bay formed by the cone of an ancient volcano. One side had eroded away enough to provide an entrance. Named Isla Partida Sur, this ridge starts geologically with the protective arm of land projecting northeast alongside La Paz and includes Isla Espíritu Santo, which we had passed in the night. After our usual hearty break fast ("I promise you'll gain at least 10 pounds," our young cook said at the outset of the voyage), we powered out of the bay and rounded the corner, approaching two small, isolated blocks of rock named Los Islotes. At their highest they reach 46 feet; the largest is perhaps 400 yards long. These are the final peaks of the submarine ridge before it plunges to the depths of the floor of the Sea of Cortez.

The larger of the Islotes had a natural arch at one side. The stark slopes were smeared with daubs of white from the swarms of birds that roost and nest here. Great frigate birds, brown-footed boobies and the local version of the Western gull (these have yellow legs and feet instead of pink) wheeled and swooped overhead, perched on narrow ledges or hunched inside the many little niches that pocked the walls of the freestanding cliffs. Frigate birds have such tiny feet that they supposedly can cling only to the slimmest of tree branches, but somehow they managed to come to rest here.

As interesting as the birds were, it was the company they kept that intrigued me. The lower rocks were alive with sea lions. One of many breeding and birthing areas for the sea lions resident in various rookeries up and down the Sea of Cortez, there were about 250 of them here, many of them mothers, most of them youngsters born within the past two months.

Perhaps a half-dozen bulls remained and had established small patches of territory on what little land there was. Occasionally I saw a juvenile male approach staked-out terrain. With much huffing and puffing and roaring, the old bull would challenge the intruder, causing the youngster to tumble off the rocks and into the water with a hurt expression on his face.

Many nursing mothers were also in evidence. Sea lions nurse their offspring for several months—unlike their cousins the elephant seals, who cut off the free milk abruptly 28 days after giving birth. Some of the young swam to our skiffs. The crew tossed out the line we used to secure the skiff to the rail of the mother ship. Deeming it a great sport, these youngsters chased after the lines while we motored around Los Islotes. They nipped after the knotted end of the rope and acted like seagoing kittens whenever we yanked the line from their grasp.

The water was clear. Close to the islets we could look down and see colorful fishes, including the magnificent moorish idol. Passengers who chose to snorkel found an amazing variety of fishes. At the rocks' edges the sea bottom dropped off dramatically, from around 30 feet to a mile and more. Some snorkelers were unnerved by the quick shift from shallow bottom to dark depths and didn't stray far from the skiffs. Nor did anyone try to climb the rocks, where groups of Sally Lightfoot crabs with their red legs and blue body tops appeared to be in command.

Sea lions claim their territory at Los Islotes, Sea of Cortez.

We had hardly left Los Islotes, powering north at midday, when a naturalist pointed excitedly to a swirling in the water and shouted, "Bryde's whale!" I was not on deck but I quickly looked out a port. It was a whale, sure enough, about as long as a gray whale but smoother; more evenly colored, with a slate color that was almost blue; thick and with very small flukes. I caught only a fleeting glance.

During the next few days we were informed that we were seeing both sei and Bryde's whales. Both inhabit these waters, but as far as I was concerned, there was no way to confirm independently which was which. It is of considerable comfort to me that Stephen Leatherwood, a senior biologist with the Hubbs Marine Research Institute in San Diego, has written that the two kinds of whales—both are classified as rorquals—look so much alike that laymen can rarely tell the difference. The sei (pronounced *say*) tends to be larger than the Bryde's whale by 4 or 5 feet; this distinction is of little help when a whale skims past the human observer. According to Richard Ellis, "Bryde's is the only baleen whale with a central and two flanking ridges on the rostrum; all other rorquals have a single ridge." The most the amateur naturalist such as myself can say about the sei and Bryde's whales is that they both look like small blue whales at casual glance.

Over the next few days we encountered several of the 100-foot-long giant blues: there was no mistaking *them*! Even from the perspective of above-water viewing, they were huge. (Those who scuba dive can sometimes see the entire beast, but I have never been inspired to don aqualung and lead weights.) But there is something about the blue whale that sets it apart from all others. It is the only whale I have met that emits an aura; it is the embodiment of the adjective *majestic*.

There were times when our persistence must have annoyed the blues while we followed—but never chased—them. They would glide through the water, gently sink below the surface, then reappear on a different tack minutes later. They never seemed to be in a hurry, nor were they ever flustered. They never changed pace. When they sounded, the huge body slid forward and down, as an endless expanse of slateblue life, always at a cadence of the whales's choosing.

CHAPTER TWELVE

Sailing with a Porpoise

THE LAND TO THE WEST LOOKED LIKE a misplaced section of the Grand Canyon. (Perhaps that's what the Sea of Cortez is: a Very Grand Canyon.) In places the Baja California peninsula along which we were sailing was sheer cliff. The strata—the layers of earth—were in contrasting colors of gray and red and brown and yellow. Once in a while a wall of this layer cake broke off abruptly into vacant canyons. Then in the distance another wall could be seen paralleling the coast again. Without apparent geological reason, an isolated hill or mesa would appear, perhaps the weathered remains of a volcano. Then the layered walls would start up again.

On the other side of the ship, open water alternated with islands, none of which appeared capable of sustaining life. The only humans to be found on them were the occasional fisherman or the traveling nature lover. Other forms of life thrived where there appeared to be nothing to thrive upon. Somehow cactus and scrub brush maintained a hold on life. As we passed by or briefly set foot on first one and then the other of these small desert islands, we learned about other creatures.

Our professional naturalists introduced the word *endemic* to our vocabulary. This adjective is used to describe a species of animal or a plant, or a variant of a species, that is peculiar to one location. A cactus

The voyage through the Sea of Cortez ends at La Paz, capital of Baja California Sur.

or a snake, a rabbit or a mouse or a lizard, can develop a peculiar physical trait that makes it different from other cacti, snakes, rabbits or lizards. This happens quite often in Baja California, especially on the islands, and we kept a lookout for endemism while visiting islands along the way.

We stopped for several hours off Punta Agua Verde on the peninsula itself, one of the places Steinbeck and Ricketts described. The fishing village consisted of a half-dozen shacks. Little brown kids ran about on the shore. Two fishermen came up to our boat for a chat with the captain. They didn't stay long. When they left, I asked the skipper what they wanted.

"They offered to sell us some turtle for dinner." He half-smiled. "I said no. I didn't think it would go over with this group of ecologists!"

A pelican goes aloft at Punta Agua Verde in the Sea of Cortez. His red breeding plumage is clearly visible on his neck.

Sensitive chap.

Most of the group went ashore to snorkel or to walk with our botany-oriented naturalist, who was hot on the trail of endemism. I had noticed some pelicans nesting on a clump of boulders just offshore, so I cornered one of the crew to take me on a solitary cruise around the rocks to get photos.

The brown pelican is only one of a number of birds found in Baja California that live off what they find in the sea. Their closest allies in the Sea of Cortez include the brown and the blue-footed boobies, both of which we saw in great numbers at Los Islotes de Partida as well as in the air elsewhere; the spectacular redbilled tropicbird, which I saw few of; the frigate, which I was introduced to for the first time in this part of the world; and three kinds of cormorants. All of them eat fish, squid and, to some extent, crustaceans.

I have a particular fondness for pelicans, which may have its roots in some unnoteworthy part of my Maine coast childhood. (One of the first couplets I learned was about the pelican with the bill that can hold more than his belly-can.) At times pelicans present a clownish appearance, perched on a wharf or looking at a person with those large, startled eyes; more often they fly in graceful formation with a half-dozen others. Though they look cumbersome and almost prehistoric, their flight is precise, each bird the same distance from the next and each changing course—up, down or sideways—with the exactness of ballet. One will drop like a rock into the water with a big splash, returning to the air bearing aloft a silvery fish destined to become lunch. On this cluster of boulders at the edge of Steinbeck's sea were perhaps a dozen of them, decked out in breeding colors that resembled a brilliant red necktie.

Pelicans were one of the creatures to have a close brush with the "silent spring" the late Rachel Carson warned us about. In the United States, DDT took a ghastly toll among the pelican population. On the California coast a severe drop in pelican populations took place over a period of several years.

They have started to make a tentative recovery. My own—admittedly unscientific—observations in the Monterey–Point Lobos area show increasing numbers of them swooping in formation off the rocky shores in search of fish or pestering the fleet at Fisherman's Wharf for a free lunch. Perhaps one secret of their survival and apparent comeback is the fact that they were not exposed to DDT in their Baja California breeding areas. Mexican agriculture is mercifully sparse in this desert region and what there is is not sophisticated enough to include the use of killer pesticides. U.S. Fish & Wildlife people have tagged young pelicans in these rookeries and have found that they have been sighted as far away from their place of birth as the San Francisco area.

The little rookery I visited at Punta Agua Verde was not as large as others on the Sea of Cortez islands, but I enjoyed my visit. It was good to see friends living where man hasn't yet developed a threat to their lives.

Sailing away from Punta Agua Verde in the early afternoon, we were treated to the sight of some more of the weird little isolated bits of rock that pop up here and there in these waters. One looked like a giant finger, only a few yards in diameter, sticking up into the air about 100 feet. Beyond, another rock formation looked like a partially submerged Monitor of Civil War fame, its "cheesebox" turret completely out of the water, a "deck" of sorts visible between waves.

Back aboard, we passed a dozen different islands during our voyage through this inland sea. We anchored off a few long enough for quick shore excursions, where we were always advised by our naturalists which endemism to watch for. One I was especially happy *not* to come across was the rattleless rattlesnake of Santa Catalina Island.

Had we gone ashore at Isla Espíritu Santo, between Cerralvo and Partida, we would perhaps have been treated to an even more dramatic, certainly more pleasant, example of endemism. This is the home of the black jackrabbit, and it's the only place where jackrabbits are black. Dr.

Krutch was among the nature writers particularly fascinated by them. He was quick to point out that there was no particular reason for a black jackrabbit. In fact, their unique coloration makes them stand out against the reddish brown soil on the island. (Kathleen Johnson Dickey refers to them as black-tailed jackrabbits; Dr. Krutch described them as all-black.) In his writing, Dr. Krutch reviewed Darwin and more recent scientific thought but could find no plausible explanation for black jackrabbits. He concluded that in science changes sometimes occur out of "caprice," and he decided that in this case, it was a "caprice of genes." He concluded that while both black jackrabbits and rattleless rattlesnakes developed by caprice, they remained changed because of a lack of a reason to change back. On the island, these endemisms are isolated from other members of the species with nonblack genes, or with rattles. Of their possible predators, the birds in the area are either magnificent fishers or hawks and falcons that hunt mice and snakes. Some eagles might occasionally go after prey as large as a rabbit, but not often enough to cause concern to Espíritu Santo's jackrabbits.

Ms. Dickey states that snakes developed rattles to keep from being trampled by the hooved animals roaming western North America. No such danger to rattlesnakes exists on Isla Santa Catalina, except for the occasional human nature-lover hoofing it between campsites.

While many of my fellow passengers enjoyed their trips ashore, I continued to find the aquatic life the most fascinating. Perhaps my log entries for part of one day toward the end of the trip will show why:

> **11:10 A.M.** Manta rays, some leaping, some swimming along the surface with their two wing tips ruffling the flat water . . . Hammerhead shark swims behind us briefly . . . Second Bryde's whale . . . Large *Turciops* (bottlenose dolphin).
>
> **12 noon.** Large school, 200-plus, of common dolphin sweep first one side of us, then the other, cross our bow in bunches of a dozen, in three and four ranks of a dozen or more; leaping sometimes straight up and falling back with a tremendous slap. Three to seven or eight leap at once in group after group. Dolphins encountered off San Jose and San Francisco islands. Some with two and three remoras attached to them.
>
> **2:20 P.M.** Large patches of krill. Anchovettis leaping about feeding on krill and dozens of brown pelicans in turn feed-

Common dolphins skim the surface of the Sea of Cortez.

ing on the silvery little fish. Patches of krill are scattered across the water so thick in some places it really looks like the Vermillion Sea of the Spanish conquistadores.

2:30 P.M. Another group of common dolphins join us, apparently feeding on anchovettis. A number of the pelicans have brilliant red breeding neck plumage.

4 P.M. Two Bryde's whales in separate locations. They surface quietly, no noisy exhaling, then slip quickly from sight again.

The dolphins created great excitement amongst us aboard ship. They must be the most captivating denizens of Earth. I have always liked to think of them as the original "people without a country," for they, like the larger whales, are citizens of the world. They travel the world's oceans without regard to borders (of course they get better protection in some waters than others).

Before the passage of the Marine Mammal Protection Act in 1972, dolphins took a chance in American waters if, as is their wont, they traveled the tropical waters of the eastern Pacific in the company of the yellowfin tuna. American tuna boats haul in about 70 percent of the yellowfin tuna; fishermen hauled in dolphins caught in their nets along with these fish. Some 400,000 dolphins died each year, not because they were the intended catch but simply because they were in the wrong place at the wrong time.

The passage of the Act has triggered some protective measures, which have had the effect of reducing the "incidental" deaths of dolphins in American waters to some 14,000 annually. In 1977 tuna captain Harold Medina introduced a change in the traditional design of the purse seine, the net in which the yellowfin tuna are caught. However, it can cost a tuna captain $100,000 or more to change to equipment that lowers dolphin mortality; rather than change their ways or stay in port, some fishermen have tried changing their American registry instead to avoid being subject to American law.

In Denmark's Faroe Islands, as well as in Japan, the annual slaughter of dolphins is still a "cultural" event. The fishermen of Iki, also in Japan, gained worldwide notoriety for their slaughter of dolphins, which they maintained was necessary because dolphins ate up their entire supply of fish.

A question that has been the subject of ongoing study for many years is why tuna and dolphins associate. The top authority on the subject is Dr. William F. Perrin, senior scientist for National Marine Fisheries Service's Southwest Fisheries Center in La Jolla. In answer to my question, he wrote: "My guess is that the bond is related in some way to foraging efficiency. We can't do much beyond guessing because it's not financially or practically feasible to experiment with tuna or dolphin in the open ocean."

Because direct experimentation is impossible, Dr. Elizabeth Vetter, who works with Dr. Perrin, has approached the question by developing mathematical models. The models are used to estimate how much food dolphins require compared to the tuna that accompany them in the tropical Pacific. In the process of building the models, she has discovered three things. The first implies that tuna might as well hang around with dolphins as not. The second implies that they shouldn't; and the third predicts a way to make it worth their while after all.

This isn't as confusing as it sounds.

First, according to Dr. Vetter, the large tuna found associating with dolphin schools are just the size that can swim optimally—for the least cost in energy—at the same speed dolphin schools choose to swim at in the wild. This means it costs the tuna nothing extra to associate with dolphins. Second, her models predict that each dolphin in the association requires five to 10 times as much food as each tuna. Since dolphin and tuna eat exactly the same things, it would seem foolish for tuna to accompany such a potentially intense competitor, even if it doesn't cost anything extra in speed.

The spinner dolphin (top center) is a prime candidate for the purse seine net because he swims with yellowfin tuna.

However, the third point that the model results show is that the tuna, simply by being smaller, escape competition because they fill their stomachs faster. Since tuna and dolphin feed by diving into patches or clumps of prey, tuna, with their smaller stomachs, fill up long before the food is gone and long before the dolphins are satisfied. Because dolphins are better than tuna at finding food, and because dolphin schools are swimming at the optimum speed for tuna anyway, it costs tuna nothing to keep up; in fact, they benefit from the association by encountering food more often than they might without the dolphins.

This is an oversimplification of Dr. Vetter's work, but it does aid in understanding this curious—and often fatal—relationship.

The waters around Baja California are home to two kinds of porpoises and nine kinds of dolphins, bringing up the old battle of what is the difference between the two.

Scientifically, they are all members of the Delphinidae family. Out of all of them, six are placed in the genus Phocaena; these are porpoises. There are small anatomical differences that are of no concern to the amateur naturalist. The NMFS call them *all* porpoises to avoid confusion with dolphinfish, which are a true fish, not a mammal. In

A pseudorca, or false killer whale, shows he is among the toothed whales.

Hawaii dolphinfish are called *mahimahi;* elsewhere they are often called *dorado.*

While dolphins and porpoises are all whales, somewhere long ago it became customary to call those less than 30 feet in length dolphins. Confusing the boundaries even more, the largest dolphin is usually called a whale; this is the orca, or killer whale. The male orca grows up to 30 feet and the female to about 23 feet. Killer whales rove in pods of five to as many as 15 and hunt for food as a cooperative effort. Their unfortunate monicker—killer—doesn't mean that they are a danger to humans; it simply means that they eat fish, seals and sea lions. They have even been seen to attack, in a group, another whale. Killer whales have also beached themselves to get at sea lions. They aren't stupid, though; they beach themselves only during a rising tide so that they can get back into the water.

Among the small whales is the harbor porpoise, which grows to between 4 and 6 feet and weighs 125 pounds; the Ganges River dolphin—

Common dolphins

or Susu—is somewhat smaller. The spotted dolphin is a close second to the harbor porpoise. The pygmy whale, at about 20 feet, is the smallest of the baleen whales (the blue is the largest).

The dolphins we saw most often around Baja California were the common dolphin, the Pacific white-sided dolphin and the bottlenose dolphin, in that order. We saw the common dolphin *(Delphinus delphis)* in large groups of several hundred romping through the Sea of Cortez. The common dolphin grows to eight feet in length and weighs up to 800 pounds; they have a brownish hourglass design on each side, making them easy to identify. (This is the same dolphin which the ancient Greeks and the Romans wrote about with such joy and reverence and depicted so delightfully in their friezes, murals, pottery and coins.)

The Pacific white-sided dolphin travels in smaller groups and is just as exuberant as the common dolphin. They grow to up to seven feet and average between 200 and 300 pounds. The bottlenose dolphin, the best-known of the dolphins as far as the human public goes, grows to 12 feet and 1,000 pounds.

Dolphins are social animals, that is, they travel in groups and interact with each other. Some chase and circle schools of fish, taking turns feeding on the school while other dolphins "herd" them so that the school cannot scatter and escape. Like some whales, the California gray included, dolphins will often assist one of their numbers in mating.

A bottlenose dolphin eyes the photographer at Sea Life Park, Oahu.

This "ménage à trois" has a nautical twist, possibly caused by the fluidity of their environment, which is that no assist is needed if both animals are moving forward. I have seen photos of dolphins mating in the usual belly-to-belly fashion while both skim ahead across the water.

Dolphins' social instincts have been known to extend to humans; stories about dolphins helping man go back to 4,000 B.C. While some are farfetched, such as those that claim dolphins have guided ships away from reefs, interactions between dolphins and people are still being documented today. Dolphins will allow people to swim with them in the wild, and they have appeared to guide people to shore, away from sharks, or to push incapacitated people shoreward (at least up to the water's surface). Dolphins must surface to breathe air and they may sense that people do, too. Dolphins have also been observed in attempts to save their own kind and other marine mammals, such as physically supporting a dead dolphin or a sea lion, as if not wanting to give up hope.

According to Dr. Kenneth S. Norris, the dean of dolphin researchers, a group of white-sided dolphins attempted to rescue a pilot whale that he had trapped during his efforts to capture a wild cetacean (he was the first, in 1958). He has been quoted as saying that white-sided dolphins swam against a line holding the pilot whale captive, as if it could be pushed free. When the pilot whale—which is actually a dolphin—was taken aboard the boat, dolphins circled the boat for some time afterward.

The possibility that dolphins possess a high degree of intelligence and have advanced capabilities of communication has fascinated a number of researchers. At this point, Dr. Norris thinks they are "high order mammals" that may lack the communicatory ability of anthropoid apes. I have heard him lecture on what he whimsically calls his "big bang theory": We all have heard the staccato squeaks and chirps—the "rusty hinge" sound, as he calls it—audible above water. He has come close to proving that under water, dolphins emit a quick sound, a "bang," that is so intense it stuns a school of fish for long enough for dolphins to prey on them.

Sound seems to be more important to dolphins—as it is for all cetaceans—than eyesight. Water, in any event, is a poor element in which to see and the position of the eyes in some cetaceans prevents them from seeing directly ahead. Dolphins use sound to determine—from its bounce—whether there is an obstacle in front and how far away it is.

Many of us, however, make dolphins out to be much more than they are. Their beguiling smile and accounts of their coexistence with humans, perhaps unfortunately, make it all too easy to anthropomorphize them.

I have watched dolphins from the decks of ships in many parts of the world. They appear out of nowhere, closing in on the ship from an angle; or they speed along beside the bow, rolling over to look us in the eyes, maintaining speed all the while; or they surf in the bow's wake, romping effortlessly, leaping high out of the water.

How can anyone watch them and not experience that most human of emotions, envy?

Getting There

PROVIDING NATURAL HISTORY EXCURSIONS has become a major industry in the past few years. Many excursions emphasize whalewatching, taking the traveler to the haunts of the great whales and the other marine mammals that share their ocean world. These cruises are not necessarily expensive nor are they exclusively for the younger person who is in top physical shape. Many voyages are under the sponsorship of organizations interested in promoting contact with and thereby knowledge of the oceans and their inhabitants. They are not out to gain profit but simply to cover their administrative costs.

My voyages to Baja California have been booked through the Oceanic Society. Three reliable organizations providing such trips are:

The American Cetacean Society
P.O. Box 2639
San Pedro, CA 90731

Oceanic Society Expeditions
Fort Mason Center, Bldg. E
San Francisco, CA 94123

Isla Santa Catalina in the Sea of Cortez is known for its barrel cactus.

Whale Center
3929 Piedmont Avenue
Oakland, CA 94611

Two commercial concerns with reputations of reliability in this field are:

H & M Landing
2803 Emerson Street
San Diego, CA 92106

Baja Expeditions, Inc.
P.O. Box 3725
San Diego, CA 92103

Several magazines regularly carry advertising about current natural history trips. These emphasize varying interests — ranging from whales to birds to the animals of the veldt — and range in price from moderate to expensive. Among the magazines, I recommend: *Natural History* (American Museum of Natural History, Central Park West at 79th, New York, New York 10024); *Smithsonian* (Smithsonian Institute, 900 Jefferson Drive, Washington, D.C. 20560); *Outdoor Photographer* (16200 Ventura Boulevard, Suite #201, Encino, CA 91436); and *Outside* (1165 North Clark Street, Chicago, Illinois 60610).

Bibliography

Beebe, William. *Zaca Venture*. New York City: Harcourt, Brace and Company, 1938.

Bryant, Peter, and Lafferty, Christopher. "The Gray Whales of Laguna Guerrero Negro." *Whalewatcher*, vol. 14, no. 4. 1980.

Dickey, Kathleen Johnson. *A Natural History Guide to Baja California*. Riverside, Ca.: (in press) 1983.

Doak, Wade. *Dolphin Dolphin*. New York: Sheridan House, 1981.

Ellis, Richard. *The Book of Whales*. New York: Alfred A. Knopf, 1985.

Fleischer, Luis A., and Beddington, J.R. "Seasonal Abundance, Reproduction and Early Mortality Rates of Gray Whales in Mexican Waters." London: Marine Resources Assessment Group, 1985.

Gardner, Erle Stanley. *Hunting the Desert Whale*. New York: William Morrow and Company, 1960.

Gilkerson, William. *The Scrimshander*. San Francisco: Troubador Press, 1975.

Gilmore, Raymond M. "Some News and Views of the Gray Whale, 1977." *Whalewatcher*, vol. 12, no. 2. 1978.

Gilmore, Raymond M. "The Friendly Whales of Laguna San Ignacio." *Terra*, vol. 15, no. 1. 1976.

Heinonen, Kurt C. "Gill Nets: O, What a Tangled Web." *Oceans*, vol. 18, no. 6. 1985.

Hilton, John W. *Hardly Any Fences*. Los Angeles: Dawson's Book Shop, 1977.

Jones, Mary Lou; Swartz, Steven L.; and Leatherwood, Stephen. *The Gray Whale*. Academic Press, Inc. (Harcourt Brace Jovanovich, Publishers), 1984.

Kaneen, Robert. "Task Force Report on Geophysical Operations." Sacramento: California State Lands Commission, 1982.

Krutch, Joseph Wood. *The Best Nature Writing of Joseph Wood Krutch*. New York: William Morrow & Company, 1969.

Lilly, John C. "The Cetacean Brain." *Oceans,* vol. 10, no. 4. 1977.

Lindsay, George. "The Friendly Whale." *Pacific Discovery,* vol. 31, no. 6. 1978.

McLeod, Samuel A. and Barnes, Lawrence G. "Gray Whales." *Terra,* vol. 22, no. 2. 1983.

McNally, Robert. *So Remorseless a Havoc.* Boston: Little, Brown, 1981.

Marine Mammal Commission. *Annual Report, 1984.* Washington, D.C.: Marine Mammal Commision, 1985.

Miller, Tom and Baxter, Elmar. *The Baja Book II.* Huntington Beach, Ca.: Baja Trail Publications, 1982.

National Marine Fisheries Service, "Biological Opinon . . . Incidental Taking." Washington, D.C.: NMFS Report, 1985.

National Marine Fisheries Service. "Endangered Species Act, Status Review, Gray Whale." Washington, D.C.: NMFS Report, 1984.

National Marine Fisheries Service. "Proposed Amendments to Regulations . . . Taking of Marine Mammals Associated With Tuna Purse Seining Operations." Washington, D.C.: NMFS Report, 1985.

National Marine Fisheries Service. "Marine Mammal Protection Act of 1972." Washington, D.C.: Annual Report, June 1984 and June 1985.

Nickerson, Thomas. *The Loss of the Ship 'Essex.'* Nantucket: The Nantucket Historical Association, 1984.

Patten, Donald R.; Samaras, William F.; and McIntyre, Diana R. "Whales, Move Over!" *Whalewatcher,* vol. 14, no. 4, 1980.

Pryor, Karen. *Lads Before the Wind.* New York: Harper & Row, 1975.

Rice, Dale W.; Wolman, Allen A.; and Brahan, Howard W. "The Gray Whale *Eschrichtius robustus.*" *Marine Fisheries Review,* vol. 46, no. 4. 1984.

Scammon, Charles M. *The Marine Mammals of the Northwestern Coast of North America.* New York: Dover Publications, 1968.

Scheffer, Victor B. *The Year of the Whale.* New York: Charles Scribner's Sons, 1969.

Slijper, Everhard J. *Whales and Dolphins.* Ann Arbor: The University of Michigan Press, 1976.

Smith, F. G. Walton. "Baja: Yesterday, Today, and Tomorrow." *Sea Frontiers,* vol. 27, no. 4. 1981.

Steinbeck, John. *The Log From the Sea of Cortez.* New York: Penguin Books, 1983.

Stonehouse, Bernard. *Sea Mammals of the World.* Middlesex: Penguin Books, 1985.

Storro-Patterson, Ron. "Gray Whale Protection." *Oceans,* vol. 10, no. 4. 1977.

Swartz, Steven L., and Jones, Mary Lou. "Mothers and Calves: Gray Whales of San Ignacio Lagoon." *Oceans,* vol. 17, no. 2, 1984.

Whipple, A. B. C. (Ed.). *The Whalers.* Alexandria, Va.: Time-Life Books, 1979.

Zwinger, Ann. *A Desert Country Near the Sea.* New York: Harper & Row, 1983.

Periodicals referred to in the bibliography are:

Oceans	The Oceanic Society Fort Mason Center, Bldg. E San Francisco, CA 94123
Pacific Discovery	California Academy of Sciences Golden Gate Park San Francisco, CA 94118
Sea Frontiers	International Oceanographic Foundation 3979 Rickenbacker Causeway Virginia Key Miami, FL 33149
Terra	The Natural History Museum Alliance of Los Angles County 900 Exposition Boulevard Los Angeles, CA 90007
Whalewatcher	The American Cetacean Society P.O. Box 2698 San Pedro, CA 90731

Index